EUROPE
a t **WAR**
1939–45

access to history

in depth

EUROPE
a t WAR
1939–45

Graham Darby

Hodder & Stoughton

A MEMBER OF THE HODDER HEADLINE GROUP

The publishers would like to thank the following individuals, institutions and companies for permission to reproduce copyright illustrations in this book:

Bettman/CORBIS: pp. 42, 53; Hulton-Deutsch Collection/CORBIS: p. 55; Oscar White/CORBIS: p. 56; CORBIS: pp. 62, 82.

The publishers would also like to thank the following for permission to reproduce material in this book:

Jonathan Cape, p. 8; Penguin, p. 53; Routledge, pp. 11, 14, 17, 35, 40, 60, 92, 99.

Every effort has been made to trace and acknowledge ownership of copyright. The publishers will be glad to make suitable arrangements with any copyright holders whom it has not been possible to contact.

Note about the Internet links in the book. The user should be aware that URLs or web addresses change regularly. Every effort has been made to ensure the accuracy of the URLs provided in this book on going to press. It is inevitable, however, that some will change. It is sometimes possible to find a relocated web page, by just typing in the address of the home page for a website in the URL window of your browser.

Orders: please contact Bookpoint Ltd, 130 Milton Park, Abingdon, Oxon OX14 4SB. Telephone: (44) 01235 827720. Fax: (44) 01235 400454. Lines are open from 9.00–6.00, Monday to Saturday, with a 24 hour message answering service. You can also order through our website www.hodderheadline.co.uk.

British Library Cataloguing in Publication Data
A catalogue record for this title is available from the British Library

ISBN 0 340 86925 9

First Published 2003
Impression number   10 9 8 7 6 5 4 3 2
Year   2009 2008 2007 2006 2005 2004

Copyright © Graham Darby, 2003

Cover photo Paul Nash, Battle of Britain © Imperial War Museum.
Produced by Gray Publishing, Tunbridge Wells, Kent
Printed in Great Britain for Hodder & Stoughton Educational, a division of Hodder Headline, 338 Euston Road, London NW1 3BH by CPI Bath.

Contents

List of Profiles

List of Maps

Preface

To the general reader

Although the *Access to History* series has been designed with the needs of students studying the subject at higher examination levels very much in mind, it also has a great deal to offer the general reader. The main body of the text (i.e. ignoring the 'Study Guides' at the ends of chapters) forms a readable and yet stimulating survey of a coherent topic as studied by historians. However, each author's aim has not merely been to provide a clear explanation of what happened in the past (to interest and inform): it has also been assumed that most readers wish to be stimulated into thinking further about the topic and to form opinions of their own about the significance of the events that are described and discussed (to be challenged). Thus, although no prior knowledge of the topic is expected on the reader's part, she or he is treated as an intelligent and thinking person throughout. The author tends to share ideas and possibilities with the reader, rather than passing on numbers of so-called 'historical truths'.

To the student reader

This title ensures the results of recent research are reflected in the text and includes features aimed at assisting you in your study of the topic at AS Level, A Level and Higher. Two features are designed to assist you during your first reading of a chapter. The *Points to Consider* section following each chapter title is intended to focus your attention on the main theme(s) of the chapter, and the issues box following most section headings alerts you to the question or questions to be dealt with in the section. The *Working on ...* section at the end of each chapter suggests ways of gaining maximum benefit from the chapter.

There are many ways in which the series can be used by students studying History at a higher level. It will, therefore, be worthwhile thinking about your own study strategy before you start your work on this book. Obviously, your strategy will vary depending on the aim you have in mind, and the time for study that is available to you.

If, for example, you want to acquire a general overview of the topic in the shortest possible time, the following approach will probably be the most effective:

1   Read Chapter 1. As you do so, keep in mind the issues raised in the *Points to Consider* section.

2 Read the *Points to Consider* section at the beginning of Chapter 2 and decide whether it is necessary for you to read this chapter.

3 If it is, read the chapter, stopping at each heading or sub-heading to note down the main points that have been made. Often, the best way of doing this is to answer the question(s) posed in the Key Issues boxes.

4 Repeat stage 2 (and stage 3 where appropriate) for all the other chapters.

If, however, your aim is to gain a thorough grasp of the topic, taking however much time is necessary to do so, you may benefit from carrying out the same procedure with each chapter, as follows:

1 Try to read the chapter in one sitting. As you do this, bear in mind any advice given in the *Points to Consider* section.

2 Study the flow diagram at the end of the chapter, ensuring that you understand the general 'shape' of what you have just read.

3 Read the *Working on ...* section and decide what further work you need to do on the chapter. In particularly important sections of the book, this is likely to involve reading the chapter a second time and stopping at each heading and sub-heading to think about (and probably to write a summary of) what you have just read.

4 Attempt the *Source-based questions* section. It will sometimes be sufficient to think through your answers, but additional understanding will often be gained by forcing yourself to write them down.

When you have finished the main chapters of the book, study the 'Further Reading' section and decide what additional reading (if any) you will do on the topic.

This book has been designed to help make your studies both enjoyable and successful. If you can think of ways in which this could have been done more effectively, please contact us. In the meantime, we hope that you will gain greatly from your study of History.

Robert Pearce

1 **Introduction**

POINTS TO CONSIDER

This chapter will introduce you to the key questions of the topic and also to the most important areas of historical debate. It will then go on to give you an outline of the book's content before taking a snapshot of the participants on the eve of the war.

1 The Key Questions

KEY ISSUE Why did Hitler lose the war he had started?

In some ways the Second World War was a rerun of the first. Arguably the country that had been responsible for the outbreak of the war in 1914 and had lost, Germany, attempted to reverse the outcome just over 20 years later. Even if we concede that the causes of the Second World War are to some extent still a matter of historical controversy, there can be no doubting the centrality of Hitler's role in any explanation. (For a full discussion of the causes of the war, the reader is referred to *Hitler, Appeasement and the Road to War 1933–41* in this *Access* series.)

Hitler clearly wished to overthrow the Treaty of Versailles, but he also had his own agenda – the uniting of all Germans and the acquisition of *Lebensraum* (living space) in the east. However, when war broke out in September 1939 it came as something of a surprise to him – after all, he had been allowed a slice of Czechoslovakia (the Sudetenland), which had never been part of Germany, so why could he not have Poland where his claim was a good one? Poland contained Germans and what had been German territory. Moreover, Hitler had done a secret deal with Stalin reminiscent of the eighteenth-century partition treaties,[1] to divide up the Polish state between Germany and the Soviet Union. As he had deprived the western democracies of the only ally capable of making a difference, Hitler could be forgiven for thinking that Britain and France would do nothing – they had given in over claims far less justifiable – but for Britain and France the issue was really Hitler, not Poland. Here was a man who could not be trusted; here was a man who had to be stopped; and eventually he was – but it would take nearly 6 years of fighting and cost millions of lives to bring this about.

ADOLF HITLER (1889–1945)

Hitler was born in Braunau in Austria on 20 April 1889. After leaving school in Linz he went to Vienna to become an artist but was unsuccessful and became a drifter. He then went to Munich and joined the German army in 1914, served in the war, and was awarded the Iron Cross First Class. After the war he joined the Nazi party and became its leader. The failure of an attempted coup (the Munich Putsch) in 1923 led to his imprisonment for 9 months at which time he wrote his semi-autobiographical work *Mein Kampf* in which he expounded his views on race and space (*Lebensraum* = 'living space'). Here he talks about Germany's need for *Lebensraum*:

> And so we National Socialists consciously draw a line beneath the foreign policy tendency of our pre-War period. We take up where we broke off six hundred years ago. We must stop the endless German movement to the south and west, and turn our gaze towards the land in the east. At long last we break off the colonial and commercial policy of our pre-War period and shift to the policy of the future. If we speak of soil in Europe, we can primarily have in mind Russia and her vassal border states.

> *from* Mein Kampf, *first published in 1925*

The Depression brought the Nazis dramatic success in the elections of 1930 and 1932, and on 30 January 1933 Hitler became Chancellor. He quickly eliminated his opponents and turned Germany into a one-party state. His attempts to reverse Versailles and unite all Germans led to rearmament, the remilitarisation of the Rhineland, *Anschluss* with Austria, the annexation of part of Czechoslovakia and an attack on Poland, which precipitated the outbreak of the Second World War in September 1939. Prior to this Hitler had made clear that the next war would be a racial war:

> Today I will once more be a prophet: if the international Jewish financiers in and outside Europe should succeed in plunging the nations once more into a world war, then the result will not be the Bolshevising of the earth and thus the victory of Jewry, but the annihilation of the Jewish race in Europe!

> *from a speech to the Reichstag, January 1939*

After defeating Denmark, Norway, Holland, Belgium and France (but not Britain) he occupied North Africa and the Balkans to rescue his fellow-dictator, Mussolini, and then turned on Russia, his principal objective, in June 1941. After dramatic initial success his soldiers were halted before Moscow in

December. In 1942 he attacked again, this time in the south in order to take the Russian oilfields; however, this campaign again came to grief in the winter – this time at Stalingrad. By 1943 it was clear that the Russian campaign had failed and with the defeat of the U-boat also in 1943, the emasculation of the *Luftwaffe* in early 1944 and the opening up of a western front in June 1944, Hitler's days were numbered. He committed suicide with his mistress Eva Braun in a bunker in Berlin on 30 April 1945. During the course of the war his appalling racial theories were put into practice and over 6 million Jews were exterminated.

The big question is, of course, how was Hitler eventually defeated – particularly given his initial dramatic success? The answer is complex and requires us to answer many other questions along the way:

- Why did Britain and France not invade Germany when Hitler was attacking Poland?
- How do we explain Hitler's success in the west in 1940?
- Why did Hitler fail to invade Britain?
- How do we explain Hitler's initial success in Russia 1941–2?
- Why did the tide turn on the Eastern Front in 1943?
- What was the economic and social impact of the war on both Nazi Germany and the Soviet Union?
- When and why did the tide turn in Western Europe?
- How serious a threat were the U-boats and how were they defeated?
- Why was D-Day such a success?
- To what extent was the defeat of Nazi Germany due to US intervention?
- How significant was Allied strategic bombing in the defeat of Hitler's Germany?
- Did intelligence play a significant part in the conflict?
- Why did Germany with virtually the entire continent at her disposal produce far fewer armaments than the Allies?
- And finally, what role did leadership and popular enthusiasm play in the outcome?

2 Historical Controversy

KEY ISSUE What are the main areas of historical debate on the Second World War in Europe?

Not surprisingly an event as complex as the Second World War has generated a number of lively debates, some of which relate to the key questions we have already asked. For instance, the question why the Allies won has been the subject of a salutary warning against falling victim to historical inevitability.[2] The idea that the Allies' overwhelming material superiority made their victory a certainty is not necessarily the case. It was at times, to use Wellington's remark about Waterloo, 'the nearest run thing'.

The collapse of France in a mere 6 weeks in 1940 has also been the subject of re-evaluation. It used to be thought that the disaster was the result of a long-term malaise, but more recently it has been seen as quite simply the result of a poor military performance in 1940. The other issue of controversy relating to France is the extent of collaboration. Can there have really been 40 million collaborators and 40 million resisters? Of course piecing together an accurate picture of resistance is in itself fraught with difficulties. What is resistance and how can we reconstruct and evaluate activities, which were, by their very nature, secret?

Over the years there has been a great deal of discussion about how close Hitler came to defeating Russia in 1941. Arguments about how the campaign was derailed by the late start or by Hitler's decision to redirect forces south in August 1941 (thereby preventing the capture of Moscow), have given way to the idea that Germany was simply not strong enough to defeat Russia – i.e. the attack was doomed from the outset. However, we might conclude that this argument smacks too much of determinism and is largely the product of hindsight.

Similarly, there is the suggestion that Britain's emphasis on pursuing a Mediterranean strategy (i.e. defeating the Germans in North Africa, and then invading Italy and possibly the Balkans) through 1942 and into 1943 postponed the opening of the Second Front, thereby condemning central Europe to conquest by the Red Army and post-war communist subjugation. It is certainly true that the Mediterranean was not an easy way into the Reich, but equally there seems to be a growing consensus that an early Second Front would not have been a success. In similar vein there is the debate about the strategy followed after D-Day. What would have been the best way to defeat Germany? Would a swift thrust to Berlin have been preferable to the broad front strategy adopted by Eisenhower? Eisenhower felt that a more gradual approach would envelop the remaining German troops and lead to the capture of the Ruhr – Germany's industrial heartland. Again, would the former approach have led to a better post-war world? The debate is ongoing, but the logistical difficulties (i.e. the difficulties in supplying and protecting, a long, narrow, exposed column) of a single thrust might well have made it impractical.

In any event the Red Army did occupy Eastern Europe and that has led to further criticism of Roosevelt and Churchill for being soft at their meeting at Yalta at the beginning of 1945 and allowing Stalin to impose communism on the occupied territories. However, the Red

Army was *in situ* (i.e. in place) and it is difficult to see what the Western Allies could have done about it.

Some historians have also criticised the Allies for adopting a policy of Unconditional Surrender at Casablanca at the beginning of 1943. Did it make the Germans fight harder? Did it make a negotiated settlement impossible? It at least had the benefit of resulting in an unambiguous outcome with no repeat of the 'stab-in-the back' myth of 1919. Germany was well and truly defeated. Even more criticism swirls around the issue of strategic bombing. Was it moral? Was it effective? And why were the extermination camps not bombed? Could the Allies have done more to prevent the Holocaust? The Holocaust remains a vibrant historical issue and this aspect of it has generated considerable unease.

Finally what sort of social impact did the war have? Did it create greater social harmony or simply mask divisions – did it help women to have greater opportunities or did they in 1945 revert to the *status quo ante bellum* (i.e. the position before the war)? There is little consensus among historians here – and the issue is not really a major concern of this book. However, if this book is able to raise as many questions as it can answer, then it will have served its purpose.

3 The Format of the Book

> **KEY ISSUE** What is the structure of the book?

a) *Blitzkrieg* 1939–41

Initially we will look at the rapid conquest of Poland, the 'Phoney War' (a period at the beginning when nothing seemed to happen – a missed opportunity for the Allies?), the impossibility of peace given Hitler's aims and personality, the Scandinavian campaign, and the crushing defeat of France. These rapid victories are seen as examples of *Blitzkrieg* tactics, but we should bear in mind the fact that the term was a journalistic invention. We also need to consider how far Hitler's success was due to the inadequacies and mistakes of the western democracies rather than German military superiority. The chapter will go on to look at the Battle of Britain (how serious was Hitler about Operation Sea Lion?) as well as Italy's intervention and the subsequent African and Balkan campaigns.

b) The Eastern Front 1941–4

Chapter 3 will look at the origins and aims of the Barbarossa campaign (Hitler's ideological obsession with *Lebensraum*) and its initial dramatic success. Despite the fact that contemporaries felt the Soviet

Union was on the verge of collapse at the end of 1941, this was to be no *blitzkrieg*, and Hitler had to launch another offensive in 1942. By this time the campaign became one of attrition, something the Germans were not prepared for, and in 1943 the tide turned. The last German success on the Eastern Front was in March 1943 and the failure of the Kursk tank battle in July marks the end of Hitler's offensive capability. Were Hitler's strategic errors to blame for this failure or was it an unwinnable campaign? In the autumn and the winter the Soviets went on the offensive and pushed the Germans back all along the front. By March 1944 the siege of Leningrad had been lifted and the prewar border of Poland had been crossed; however, the greatest advance was in the south where the Ukraine was reconquered and the Romanian border breached. The chapter also looks at the social and economic impact of the war on Nazi Germany and the Soviet Union and its contribution to the latter's success and the former's failure.

c) The Tide Turns in the West 1942–4

Chapter 4 will look at the defeat of Rommel in North Africa, US intervention in that theatre (Operation Torch), the invasion of Italy (not the 'soft underbelly' that Churchill had predicted) and the build-up to Operation Overlord. It will then go on to look at the Battle of the Atlantic – the defeat of the U-boat was essential for the launching of the invasion of France – and finish by looking at the controversial topic of strategic bombing, the Allied bombing campaign of Germany.

d) Behind the Lines

Chapter 5 will look at how the Germans governed and controlled their Empire – how occupied territory was exploited, how native peoples were treated (with barbaric cruelty), how there was both collaboration and resistance, and how Hitler's racial theories led inexorably to the 'Final Solution'. It will also will look at important topics that are common to the whole war, such as the relative importance of technology, intelligence, alliances and strategy.

e) Total Defeat 1944–5

Chapter 6 will look at the continuing Russian success on the Eastern Front (by far the most important theatre) as well as the success of D-Day and the opening of the second front in France in June 1944. Despite the failure of Operation 'Market Garden' (the attempt to cross the Rhine by taking a series of Dutch bridges – the one too far being Arnhem) and the initial success of the 'Battle of the Bulge', by 1945 the Third Reich was disintegrating rapidly and the end came by May. Was Eisenhower right to pursue a broad front strategy and did the Russians deserve to take Berlin?

f) Conclusions

The book will conclude with a summary discussion of why the Allies won before going on to take a brief look at the cost and consequences of the war – the huge numbers of deaths and the division of Europe between the capitalist west and the communist east.

4 The Protagonists on the Eve of the War

> **KEY ISSUE** What were the relative strengths of Germany, Britain and France in 1939?

Despite the fact that the major European powers had begun rearmament programmes in the 1930s as tensions rose, none of them was ready for war in 1939. Germany's initial victories gave the false impression that the Germans enjoyed superior numbers and were in a state of high readiness – they did not, and they were not. In fact all Hitler's plans were geared to 1942–3,[3] though increasingly he came to fear that his rearmament lead would be whittled away, that time was running against him. Because of this he came to welcome the war.

The German army (the *Wehrmacht*) possessed nearly 4 million men and 3000 tanks but it lacked motorised transport and was to be heavily dependent on horses throughout the war. The Navy (*Kriegsmarine*) was no match for the Royal Navy though the airforce (*Luftwaffe*) with 2500 modern aircraft did have a numerical advantage. Where the Germans scored highly was in terms of planning and preparation; in addition, air and ground forces were well integrated and officers were trained to take the initiative.

The French army was nearly 5 million strong and also possessed 3000 tanks; however, much of its equipment was obsolete and it was designed to fight a static war (behind the Maginot Line) rather like 1914–18. The French navy was strong but its air force was very much the weak link with fewer than 1000 modern planes. The British Army was small in comparison with less than a million men and about 600 tanks. The British generals also anticipated a fairly static campaign – a slow advance on a continuous front as in the Great War. The Royal Navy was in reasonable shape and the RAF had recently been improved; it had nearly 2000 planes, though only half were modern.

In short, the two sides were roughly equally matched at the outbreak of war though the Germans were prepared to fight it at a much faster pace. They did not, however, use the term *Blitzkrieg* – this was a term first employed by western journalists to describe the rapidity of the Polish campaign in 1939.

Table 1 War Potential of the Great Powers *c.* 1937[4]

State	Population (millions)	Nat income ($ billons)	% On defence	Relative war potential
USA	129	68	1.5	41.7
Germany	68	17	23.5	14.4
USSR	167	19	26.4	14.0
UK	47	22	5.7	10.2
France	41	10	9.1	4.2
Japan	70	4	28.2	3.5
Italy	43	6	14.5	2.5

Note. Relative war potential is calculated by taking into account the size of the population and the strength of the economy.

Table 2 Weapons Production 1939[5]

State	Aircraft	Tanks	Artillery
USA	5856	–	–
Germany	8295	1300	2000
USSR	10382	2950	17439
UK	7940	1399	1400
Japan	4467	1023	?

References

1. Poland had been partitioned out of existence in a series of partition treaties in 1772, 1792 and 1795 signed between Russia, Austria and Germany's predecessor Prussia. She had not re-emerged until 1918 just after the Russian Revolution.
2. See especially R. Overy, *Why the Allies Won* (Jonathan Cape, 1995).
3. Graham Darby, *Hitler, Appeasement and the Road to War 1933–41* (Hodder, 1999), p. 101.
4. S.P. MacKenzie, *The Second World War in Europe* (Longman, 1999), p. 7.
5. R. Overy, *Why the Allies Won*, pp. 331–2.

Working on Chapter I

This chapter is essentially introductory. Its main objective is to introduce students to the important questions that are thrown up by the Second World War and to the main areas of historical debate. The format of the book gives some idea of where these matters will be addressed; however, in such a short work it is just not possible to do other than touch upon many of them – this is essentially a first stop: for greater depth students are advised to move on to the larger works, several of which are mentioned in the bibliography.

2 Blitzkrieg 1939–41

POINTS TO CONSIDER

This chapter will look at Hitler's rapid success in Poland and Western Europe, his setback with Britain and his intervention in Africa and the Balkans. You should consider why he was so successful and whether or not these were the campaigns he really wanted to be fighting.

KEY DATES

1939	1 September	Hitler invades Poland
	3 September	Britain and France declare war on Germany
1940	9 April	Hitler invades Norway and Denmark
	10 May	Hitler invades Holland, Belgium and France. Churchill replaces Chamberlain as PM
	15 May	Holland surrenders
	27 May	Belgium surrenders
	10 June	Italy declares war on Britain and France
	22 June	France capitulates
	10 July	Battle of Britain begins
	7 September	the 'Blitz' begins
	September	Italy invades Egypt
	October	Italy invades Greece
1941	February	Formation of the Afrika Korps
	11 March	Lend-Lease bill signed in the USA
	6 April	Hitler invades Yugoslavia and Greece
	31 May	British defeated in Crete

1 The Invasion of Poland

> **KEY ISSUE** Why was the campaign over so quickly?

Operation White, the codename for the invasion of Poland, was finalised as early as 15 June 1939 and was implemented, after some vacillation by Hitler, on 1 September. After a slight delay brought about by a lack of coordination between Britain and France, and after considerable pressure on Chamberlain in the House of Commons, the two democracies declared war on Germany on 3 September. Britain and France did not go to war to protect Poland, but to prevent German domination of Europe. Thus Poland was the occasion for the war, rather than its cause.

The Allied aim at this stage was not the total defeat and surrender of Germany but Hitler's replacement by another leader and a

European settlement, which would restore Czechoslovakia pre-Munich yet take some account of the modifications to the Versailles Treaty that had occurred over time. The Allies went to war in 1939 with great reluctance though public opinion had undergone a major change between the summers of 1938 and 1939. There was now considerable patriotic solidarity and a universal feeling that Hitler had to be stopped by force.

Of course it was accepted that little could be done for the Poles – it was realised that they stood little chance and that they would eventually be overrun. The French had promised the Poles they would invade Germany within 15 days were war to break out, but General Gamelin had no intention of honouring that promise. Allied strategy was to wage a defensive war and build up strength, to buy time so that rearmament could go on apace and large armies be put together, in the belief that the war was bound to be a long one – a strategy very much rooted in the experience of the Great War where defence was easier than attack and where victory came by attrition and superior numbers. This strategy only looks mistaken in the light of what happened in May 1940. At the time there was much to be said for it, as British and French strength was increasing faster than that of the Germans. Indeed Hitler too believed that time was not on his side – his generals feared an attack in the west, which is why he was concerned to achieve a very rapid victory in Poland.

Gambling that Britain and France would not attack immediately, Hitler denuded the Western Front and threw everything at the Poles. Leaving aside the abiding image of cavalry charging tanks, which is not wholly accurate, it is still the case that the Poles did not stand a chance. The odds were stacked against them: 2 million men against 1 million (mobilisation had not been fully implemented on the advice of Britain and France so as not to provoke Hitler!); and 2000 airplanes against less than half that number (and most of those were obsolete and destroyed on the ground). In addition, the Poles adopted the mistaken policy of a forward defence and spread their army thinly along their long border. This was a political decision not a military one; the objective was to hold territory at all costs, but it would have been better to keep the army back and concentrate it. This strategy played into German hands. They employed a combination of a straight punch and pincer movement. The tanks raced ahead, the motorised infantry consolidated their pathway and the infantry occupied territory and mopped up. The *Luftwaffe* controlled the skies and the *Wehrmacht* advanced with such speed that the Polish army was divided into pockets and surrounded.

Then on 17 September the Soviets invaded from the east in accordance with the Nazi–Soviet Pact of 23 August (but this did not elicit a further declaration of war by the western democracies). Warsaw capitulated on 27 September and all resistance ceased by 6 October. It was a comprehensive victory for Hitler and at a cost of only 45,000

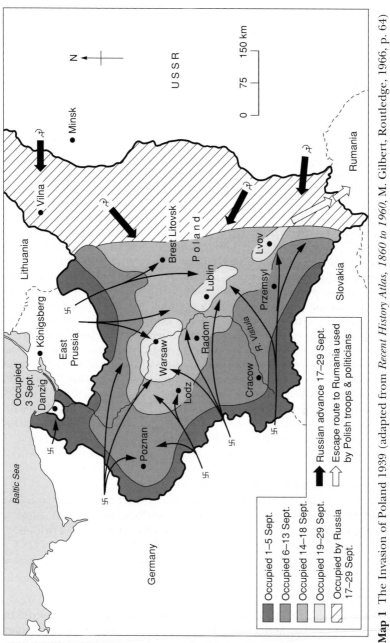

Map 1 The Invasion of Poland 1939 (adapted from *Recent History Atlas, 1860 to 1960*, M. Gilbert, Routledge, 1966, p. 64)

casualties (the Poles had 200,000). Moreover, it was the first example of what journalists called *Blitzkrieg* tactics – fast-moving attacks delivered by a small but effective tank force, supported by overwhelming air power.

The big question is, of course, why did the French fail to launch an attack in the west? After all it was clearly a missed opportunity as the Germans had completely stripped their Rhine defences. The reason would seem to be the defensive strategy previously mentioned. In addition, the Allies – Britain and France – were not in fact ready – mobilisation was proceeding slowly and in any event there was also the misplaced hope that an economic blockade would bring Germany to her knees without offensive action – without any actual fighting. This was based on the (erroneous) assumption that the German economy was already at full stretch and about to collapse.

Poland was now wiped from the map and its territory divided between Nazi Germany and the Soviet Union. Stalin had in effect given Hitler a free hand in the west while he came to dominate (and eventually take over) the Baltic States (Latvia, Lithuania and Estonia). He also fought a dogged winter war with Finland. Meanwhile in an address to the *Reichstag* on 6 October Hitler generously offered peace, but the Allies were not taken in. A peace settlement without any concessions would no doubt have suited the *Führer*, but he must have realised it was unrealistic and simultaneously ordered preparation for an immediate major offensive in the west. It was initially ordered to begin on 12 November but was postponed 29 times before the actual date of 10 May. This was not due to the opposition of his generals (though many were aghast), but because of the weather and because of a series of leaks – at times due to intelligence, at times due to accident.[1] Ironically successive postponements had the effect of undermining intelligence as to the actual date and successive leaks gave the wrong impression about the strategy – and it gave the Germans the opportunity to improve and alter their plan.

2 The War in the West

KEY ISSUES Why were British and French land forces (and those of Holland and Belgium) so easily defeated and why did Britain not make peace?

a) The Phoney War

The 'Phoney War' was aptly named. Britain and France braced themselves for massive aerial bombardment and colossal civilian casualties: coffins were made ready, children were evacuated … and nothing happened. The RAF dropped a few leaflets but that was about it. On the Western Front the armies faced each other from behind defences, but apart from occasional patrolling, little occurred. An uneasy calm ensued: only at sea was there real conflict.

Yet the two sides were not idle – they both planned for victory. The Allies were preparing for an extended struggle. Given the belief in the inviolability of the Maginot Line, the Allies correctly assumed that Hitler would attack through the Low Counties. However, they did not spend these months well – no uniform command structure was agreed upon while the timidity of the Dutch and Belgian governments made proper provision for the defence of these countries impossible. The Anglo-French strategy was basically to commit the most effective force to an advance deep into Belgium once Germany attacked – however, this strategy lacked any flexible response to anything unexpected – while the Belgians refused to cooperate and the Dutch planned to retreat north away from the Allied advance. Hitler did initially plan an attack in the north but once that plan became compromised by captured documents, his inclination to push through the Ardennes in the south was given form by General von Manstein. His generals urged caution, but Hitler's confidence carried the day: he believed he could defeat France and make Britain negotiate, but prior to this attack he was sidetracked into a Scandinavian expedition.

b) The Scandinavian Diversion

Hitler's Grand Admiral, Erich Raeder, had urged Hitler throughout the autumn and winter of 1939 to pre-empt the allies and occupy Norway. He wanted bases for his navy, and its occupation would also secure Germany's iron ore supplies from Sweden, which had to come via Norwegian waters in winter. Preoccupied by the attack in the west, Hitler did not really become interested in the project until early 1940 when plans were drawn up. Irritated by the Royal Navy's capture of prisoners from the German ship, *Altmark*, in Norwegian waters, Hitler took the decision in March 1940 to launch an invasion in early April. At about this time the Germans became aware of Allied plans.

The French had become increasingly worried that the blockade strategy was being completely undermined by Soviet aid to Germany and contemplated assisting the Finns in their war with Russia. Aid to Finland could only go through Norway and Sweden and such an action would make it possible to cut the iron ore supplies to Germany. Britain, wary of confronting the Russians, favoured the latter plan and when the Finns gave up the fight in March the plan was changed to mining Norwegian waters.

At this point Hitler struck – Denmark was rapidly and bloodlessly occupied on 9 April (she capitulated the next day) and Norway was invaded. The Norwegians decided to fight and Britain and France sent forces. The Norwegian invasion did not go fully according to

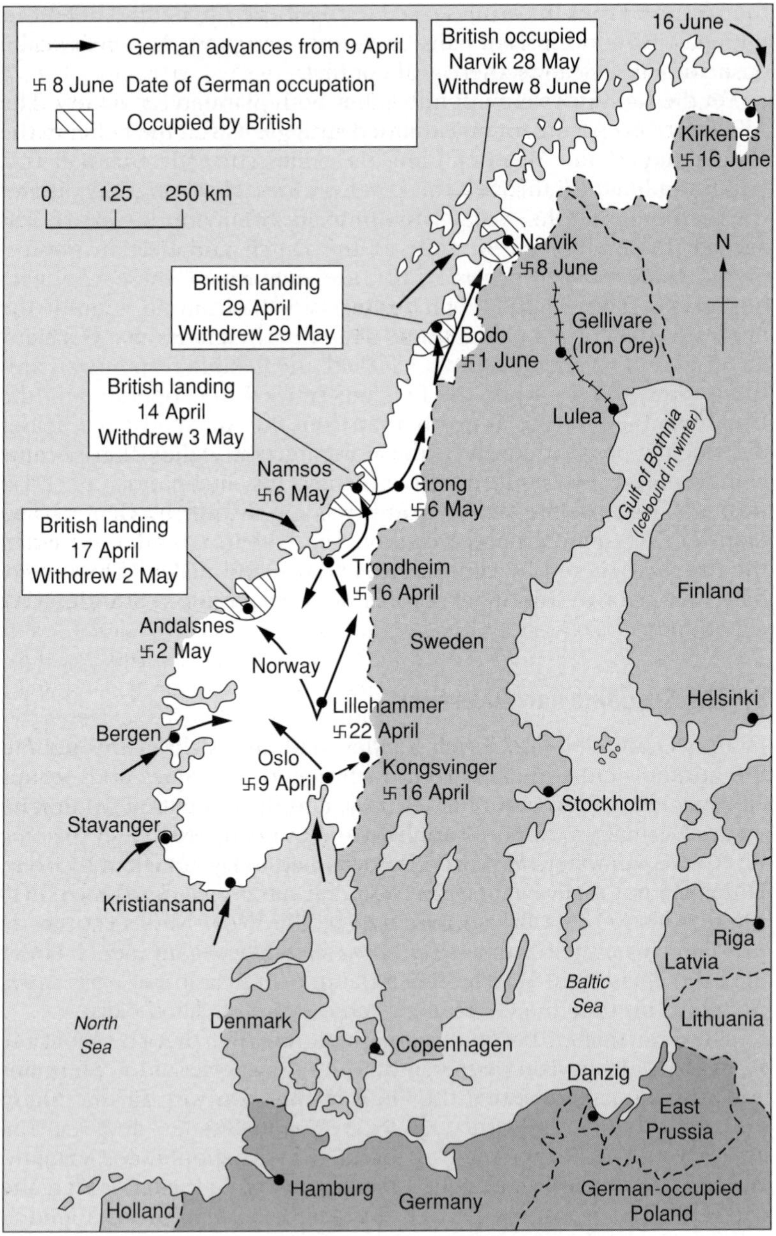
German advances from 9 April
卐 8 June Date of German occupation
Occupied by British
0 125 250 km
British occupied Narvik 28 May Withdrew 8 June
16 June
Kirkenes 卐 16 June
Narvik 卐 8 June
N
British landing 29 April Withdrew 29 May
Bodo 卐 1 June
Gellivare (Iron Ore)
Lulea
British landing 14 April Withdrew 3 May
Namsos 卐 6 May
Grong 卐 6 May
Gulf of Bothnia (Icebound in winter)
British landing 17 April Withdrew 2 May
Trondheim 卐 16 April
Finland
Andalsnes 卐 2 May
Sweden
Norway
Lillehammer 卐 22 April
Helsinki
Bergen
Oslo 卐 9 April
Kongsvinger 卐 16 April
Stockholm
Stavanger
Kristiansand
Riga
Latvia
Baltic Sea
North Sea
Denmark
Lithuania
Copenhagen
Danzig
East Prussia
Hamburg
Germany
German-occupied Poland
Holland

Map 2 The Norwegian Campaign 1940 (adapted from *Recent History Atlas, 1860 to 1960*, M. Gilbert, Routledge, 1966, p. 67)

plan for the Germans – the Royal Navy got the upper hand and the Germans lost a lot of ships – but thanks to air superiority, the imaginative use of air transport, good inter-service cooperation, better meteorological information and Allied incompetence, the Germans prevailed. The Allied operation was seriously mismanaged – the expeditionary force was without air cover, insufficiently supplied and poorly led. The Allies did establish a toehold at Narvik but this had to be abandoned in June, and Norway capitulated on 10 June. Long before this, on 10 May, the failure of this expedition had led to the fall of Chamberlain's government and his replacement by Winston Churchill. However, the 10 May was significant for another reason; on that day Hitler launched his long anticipated attack on the west.

c) The Fall of France

As we have already indicated, the Germans planned that Army Group B would attack in the north as something of a diversion to draw the Allies away from France while Army Group A would thrust through the hilly wooded Ardennes, which many considered unsuitable for tanks and which had been left unprotected by the Maginot Line. The Panzer (armoured units) divisions would then race to the coast gambling that their exposed flanks would not be attacked, so that the main French and British forces would be trapped, cut off from communications, unable to retreat and would be sandwiched between two German armies. By May 1940 the forces deployed on each side were roughly equal (the Allies had 138 divisions, the Germans 136). Remarkably this plan worked – it was remarkable because not only did the plan contain the element of surprise, but the attack itself was completely unexpected: the French were not expecting an invasion until 1941.

The Germans launched the campaign on 10 May when Army Group B attacked. Immediately General Gamelin, the French commander, moved the BEF (the British Expeditionary Force) and the French 1st and 7th armies north – this represented one-third of the army, most of its tanks and his reserve. Then on 12 May, out of the blue, the Panzers of Army Group A came crashing out of the Ardennes forest and achieved an immediate breakthrough. Attempts to attack the flanks were ordered but never occurred and the whole fiasco revealed the weakness of the Allied air force and the slowness of the Allied command and control structure. By 20 May the Panzers had reached the sea – aided by German command of the skies and a crisis of confidence in the French High Command. Already on 15 May, the day Holland capitulated, Churchill noticed on his visit to the French government that officials were burning documents, a sure sign of impending evacuation. On 19 May, Gamelin was replaced by Weygand as commander-in-chief, but by the last week of May the BEF and the French 1st Army were boxed in by the coast at Dunkirk and the British took the decision to evacuate as many soldiers as possible.

Between 27 May, the day Belgium surrendered, and 4 June, 338,000 soldiers, a third of whom were French were taken off the beaches by a vast array of assorted vessels, – warships, coastal steamers and even pleasure boats and yachts. The 'miracle of Dunkirk' was an evacuation on a scale not envisaged by either the British or the Germans until it happened and it needs some explanation. The British were let off the hook because von Rundstedt halted his tanks on 24 May, a decision that perhaps only appears a technical mistake with hindsight. He did this for a variety of reasons – half his tanks had broken down and the other half needed maintenance. He also thought the terrain around Dunkirk was quite unsuitable for tanks. He believed that his priority was to turn south and defeat France and Goering boasted that his *Luftwaffe* would now finish the job. However, a combination of poor weather (rain and fog) and the RAF thwarted his ambitions. Moreover it is sometimes forgotten that the French 1st Army fought a valiant rearguard action that also made the evacuation possible.

Although the 'Dunkirk Spirit' became part of British popular mythology there can be no disguising the fact that the British army had suffered a massive defeat. Britain had abandoned not only her equipment but had left her French and Belgian allies to their fate. General Weygand subsequently decided to make a stand along a front from the Somme to the Aisne but he was now outnumbered two to one. The battle only lasted 5 days, from the 5 June to 10 June, before the Germans broke through. Paris fell on the 14 June and on 16 June Marshal Pétain, the ageing First World War hero of Verdun, took over the government and accepted defeat. An armistice was signed on 21 June and came into effect the following day. Two days later an armistice was signed with Italy. Mussolini had finally mustered up the courage to declare war on 10 June but the Italian army had failed to make any progress when it invaded southern France. Hitler occupied the whole of northern France and the Atlantic coast, while the unoccupied zone was ruled by Pétain from Vichy. The Vichy government also retained control of the French Empire and the French Navy.

The defeat of France in 6 weeks was an astonishing success and it too requires some explanation. It was once widely believed that French morale was so low, that the third Republic was so rotten, that France was on the verge of collapse anyway. But this was not the case. The French collapse was first and foremost a military defeat.[2] Undoubtedly the French army was badly trained, badly equipped and badly led – it had not been modernised; but we must not overdo these points since it had little difficulty in resisting the Italian invasion. It remains hard to strike a balance between how far this campaign was won by the Germans (who used their armour brilliantly) or lost by the French (who appear to have committed a number of mistakes). Here we can point the finger at Gamelin who had squandered his reserve. He had left too many men on the Maginot Line who were not utilised

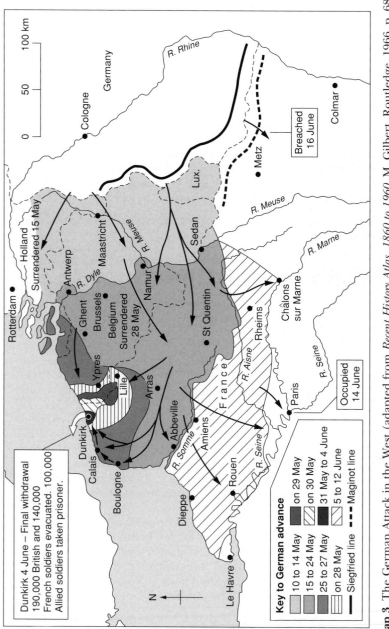

Map 3 The German Attack in the West (adapted from *Recent History Atlas, 1860 to 1960*, M. Gilbert, Routledge, 1966, p. 68)

(two-fifths of the army!), and he did not have a proper command structure – which would have facilitated quick communication. So a poorly led and badly coordinated Allied force (the British must share some of the blame too) was pierced at a critical point and was never again able to regain even its balance, let alone the initiative.

We must conclude that it was a plan well executed and incompetently opposed. But there is no doubt that the French government was weak and showed little resolve. Moral authority and executive capacity both disappeared and military defeat turned into political collapse. Essentially Hitler's military successes were based on his preparedness to take the adventurous and unexpected course. He was fortunate that military thinking lagged behind military technology. Moreover, whereas the Allies were cautious and conservative, Hitler was an impatient man who was psychologically predisposed to adopt daring and mobile strategies. What was he going to do next? On 18 June Churchill thought he knew:

> the battle of France is over. I expect that the Battle of Britain is about to begin.

WINSTON CHURCHILL (1874–1965)

Born at Blenheim Palace, a direct descendant of the Duke of Marlborough, Churchill went into the army, but after serving in the Sudan and in the Boer War (where he was briefly captured), he became a Conservative MP in 1900. He switched to the Liberals in 1906 and by 1910 he was Home Secretary. At the outbreak of the war he was First Lord of the Admiralty (since 1911), but resigned over the Dardanelles fiasco (1915). After a spell fighting in France he returned to government in 1917. He switched back to the Conservatives in the 1920s and served as Chancellor of the Exchequer from 1924 to 1929. However, by the 1930s he was on the back-benches in the political wilderness with the reputation as someone who was a bit of a maverick. It looked as though his career was over; however, his attacks on Hitler and appeasement led to his recall to government on the outbreak of war in 1939.

He succeeded Chamberlain as Prime Minister in May 1940. This heralded the beginning of his 'walk with destiny' for which he considered his earlier life a preparation and he came to embody the bulldog spirit of resistance that characterised 'Britain Alone'. Addressing the House of Commons 3 days after becoming Prime Minister, he stated:

> We have before us an ordeal of the most grievous kind. We have before us many, many long months of struggle and of suffering. You ask, what is our policy? I will say: It is to wage war, by sea, land and

> air, with all our might and with all the strength that God can give us;
> to wage war against a monstrous tyranny, never surpassed in the
> dark, lamentable catalogue of human crime. That is our policy. You
> ask, what is our aim? I can answer in one word: It is victory, victory
> at all costs, victory in spite of all terror, victory, however long and
> hard the road may be; for without victory, there is no survival.[3]

During the war he worked tirelessly, clocked up 150,000 miles of
travel and worked hard to maintain a British voice in the Grand
Alliance. For many he was the man who won the war for Britain,
though a war leader was no longer required in 1945. Defeated at
the polls in that year, he returned as Prime Minister, 1951–5.
Known in his later years as 'the greatest living Englishman', he
won the Nobel Prize for Literature in 1953 (especially for his six-
volume history of the war) and was awarded honorary US
citizenship in 1963.

d) The Battle of Britain

Even during the early phase of the attack on France in May, Hitler
often stated he just wanted a peace settlement with Britain – not an
invasion. On 2 June he told a group of officers he hoped Britain
would accept a reasonable peace – based on his mastery of the continent – which would leave him free to pursue his 'really great task' of
crushing the Soviet Union. Indeed the British cabinet did discuss the
possibility of a peace settlement at the end of May and some were in
favour of negotiation (e.g. Lord Halifax); however, Churchill was
implacably opposed and his attitude proved to be decisive; he proved
to be the right man at the right time. His pre-war anti-Hitler stance
now conferred on him a reputation for prescience (foreknowledge or
foresight) and wisdom and his speeches proved to be inspirational. In
the first as Prime Minister he had promised, in those memorable
words, 'I have nothing to offer but blood, toil, tears and sweat'. In the
House of Commons on 4 June he stated:

> We shall go on to the end. We shall fight in France, we shall fight on
> the seas and oceans, we shall fight with growing confidence and grow-
> ing strength in the air, we shall defend our island, whatever the cost may
> be. We shall fight on the beaches, we shall fight on the landing grounds,
> we shall fight in the fields and in the streets, we shall fight in the hills;
> we shall never surrender …

On 18 June he declared:

> The whole fury and might of the enemy must very soon be turned on
> us. Hitler knows that he will have to break us in this island or lose the
> war. If we can stand up to him, all Europe may be free, and the life of

the world may move forward into broad, sunlit uplands; but if we fail, then the whole world, including the United States, including all that we have known and cared for, will sink into the abyss of a new dark age made more sinister and perhaps more protracted by the lights of a perverted science. Let us therefore brace ourselves to our duties and so bear ourselves that if the British Empire and its Commonwealth last for a thousand years, men will still say 'This was their finest hour'.

The rejection of peace did lead to Britain's 'finest hour', but some historians have questioned the wisdom of ruling out peace since the war exhausted Britain and pretty much finished her off as a great power.[4] Churchill was a romantic who revelled in the drama of a heroic cause – but Britain could at best only survive, it was impossible to see how she could win the war. And this was the view that Hitler took – he felt sure Britain would make peace; he was astonished when she did not. He renewed his peace offer on 19 July – he would be master of Europe and he would leave the British Empire intact. He was exasperated when his offer was rejected and he came to realise that he would get nowhere as long as Churchill was Prime Minister – he would have to force Great Britain to make peace. Invasion, however, was not really on his agenda – it was to be a last resort, so he gave Operation Sea Lion, as the invasion plan was called, a very low priority and believed it would not be necessary. In any event Admiral Raeder had strong reservations about it and Jodl believed an air campaign would suffice to bring peace.

Hitler had ordered some preliminary planning for Sea Lion on 2 July and on 16 July he issued a directive for an invasion on 15 September 'if necessary'.[5] The German Navy was in no position to protect an invasion force – losses in the Norwegian campaign had not been made good and Churchill had attacked the French fleet at Oran to prevent its requisition – therefore air supremacy was essential. The army was justifiably confident and there is no doubt that, had it landed, it would not have faced well-organised opposition. Therefore whether or not Britain was invaded would depend upon whether the *Luftwaffe* could wear down the RAF to the point where it could not protect the ships of the Royal Navy trying to stop the invasion, nor seriously interfere with German vessels crossing the channel. This then is how this unique conflict – a battle in the air – came about.

On paper the *Luftwaffe* had considerable numerical superiority with about 2500 planes to the RAF's 1000. However, these figures are deceptive: half the German planes were vulnerable bombers with a limited range and a limited bomb load (Germany had not developed long-range heavy bombers) and although in the *Messerschmidt* Bf-109 the *Luftwaffe* possessed an excellent fighter, it too had a limited range – only about 30 minutes over England (10 minutes over London) and was unsuitable for escort work. In addition, the *Luftwaffe* had to move to new airfields in France and Belgium that did not possess the maintenance infrastructure to keep the planes airworthy.

The RAF, on the other hand, did possess the maintenance structure to keep the planes airworthy – and its pilots could spend much longer in the air. Moreover, if they bailed out they could fight again, whereas the German pilots became prisoners. In addition, in the Hurricane and especially the Spitfire, the RAF had two fighters that could give the Bf-109 a run for its money. But Britain did have fewer planes and pilots – the 'few' was in fact the right word. Although aircraft production was good (at over 400 per month it exceeded that of Germany) pilots could not be trained that quickly. Given the RAF's numerical inferiority, what proved crucial was a revolutionary new warning system: RDF – radio direction finding, better known as radar. This British invention (and the construction of over 50 strategically placed stations) enabled the RAF to concentrate its forces on the enemy rather than spread them out or waste time patrolling. Radar could pick up enemy aircraft at about 75 miles' distance and give some idea of numbers and altitude so that sufficient fighters could be scrambled in time to meet them. However, radar was just part of a sophisticated integrated control and warning system, which included 1000 observer corps posts, radio telephones and operations rooms – all under the watchful control of Air Chief Marshal, Sir Hugh Dowding.

In this campaign (and in sharp contrast to the *Wehrmacht*) the *Luftwaffe* did not really seem to have a clear strategy – other than to bring Britain to her knees – and seemed to proceed by improvisation. Of course to some extent the primary aim was to force peace, rather than the secondary one, carry out an invasion. This improvisation is reflected in the phases of the battle that historians have identified.

i) 10 July–early August 'Channel Battle' (*Kanalkampf*)
ii) 13–18 August 'Operation Eagle'; 19–23 August a pause; 24 August–6 September attack on Fighter Command's airfields
iii) 7–30 September – the Battle of London[6]

In fact the German airforce had been set a colossal task: the *Luftwaffe* had to deliver the circumstances for a victory before the army and navy had even been committed. Herman Goering, Air Minister and Chief of the *Luftwaffe*, made light of this but many professionals were perturbed. The Germans began in July by attacking shipping in the channel and the ports. This carried on for about a month and was not very effective; it saw the withdrawal of the rather slow JU 87 *Stuka* dive bomber (good at strafing refugees, but no match for Hurricanes and Spitfires).

Operation Eagle was a much more serious and effective affair – by the end of August the RAF was losing more planes than it could replace, twice as many pilots as were coming out of training, and six out of seven airfields in the south-east were out of action. Dowding was pessimistic and it was thought that the RAF could only carry on for about a fortnight at this rate. Clearly a consistent policy of targeting the airbases might well have succeeded, but on 7 September the

Luftwaffe switched to bombing London. This turned out to be a major tactical error and enabled the RAF to recover. It is impossible to be absolutely sure of the chief reason for this switch, but clearly there were a number of factors. It would seem that Kesselring thought that the battle was all but won and that a terrifying attack on London would be the last straw, break British morale, and force the British government to sue for peace.[7] This did not happen and from 11 September Hitler began to postpone the invasion until in October it was postponed indefinitely. This was Hitler's first setback.

For Britain the margin of victory was narrow, but it was enough. Throughout the conflict claims about enemy losses were grossly inflated (by both sides) to boost morale. However, there is no doubt that the RAF got the better of the *Luftwaffe* – the RAF lost just under 800 planes, the *Luftwaffe* in excess of 1300. The Battle of Britain was won by a small elite of 2945 RAF pilots of whom 507 were killed and 500 wounded. As Churchill put it, 'never in the field of human conflict has so much been owed by so many to so few'. But from the aircraft factory worker through to fighter command right up to Dowding, it was a collective effort that involved a great many more.

Was Hitler ever serious about invasion? Most of those who knew him contended he was not – it was a psychological weapon to break British morale and free him for his major task, the invasion of Russia. Of course the army took it seriously and drew up detailed invasion plans, men were assigned and trained; the navy assembled barges, tugs and other craft, and the SS drew up lists of undesirables who were to be arrested – but Hitler was half-hearted; he wanted a peace with fellow Aryans. British defiance was an inconvenience and deflected him from his major racial task: the conquest of *Lebensraum* from 'inferior' peoples.

Subsequently the *Luftwaffe* switched to a heavy night bombing offensive against military and economic targets in major cities – a campaign better known as the Blitz. Although the Germans dropped 35,000 tons of bombs between September 1940 and May 1941 (over half of it on London) the widespread panic and high death rate that had been predicted did not materialise – indeed a cheery and defiant London was a crucial image of Britain at war. A major effort at debunking the 'spirit of the Blitz' has tried to focus on less than heroic episodes (panic in Coventry and Southampton for instance); however, any explanation of the Blitz has to work through the propaganda and weigh up the bravery, endurance and defiance against the panic and cowardice – it seems the former well outweighs the latter.[8]

Bombing raids and potential invasion were not the only, nor perhaps even the most serious, threats Britain faced. Her ability to feed her population and maintain her war machine depended upon control of the sea, but the Battle of the Atlantic, a phrase Churchill coined in March 1941, is the subject of another chapter (see page 61).

Little, not even Churchill's rhetoric, could disguise the fact that though Germany had not defeated Britain, then there was certainly no possibility of Britain defeating Germany. What sustained Churchill was a serene confidence that the USA would come into the war – but his confidence was not well founded: President Roosevelt did not want to see a fellow democracy defeated, but he was not preparing for war. Initially, Roosevelt did a deal – destroyers for bases – in September 1940, but this was insufficient to keep Britain going. Accordingly in 1941, Roosevelt came up with the Lend-Lease Bill whereby the USA would supply the arms Britain needed and arrangements for repayment would be made later. As he explained to the American people, it was like a man who lends his neighbour a garden hose to put out a fire – the emergency takes precedence over the matter of repayment. Roosevelt was able to counter isolationist sentiment by cleverly suggesting that only by supporting Britain would the USA be able to stay out of the war. By 1945 Britain had received over $22 billion of aid.[9] Of course Churchill was to be vindicated in his stance not by any great foresight but by two decisions taken by Adolf Hitler – the invasion of Russia and the declaration of war on the USA – both of which are the subject of the next chapter.

e) Africa and the Balkans

Mussolini's belated declaration of war in June 1940 had opened up a new theatre of operations in the Mediterranean. In September, Marshal Rodolfo Graziani in Libya had finally begun a cautious push into Egypt. Although the British Commander, Sir Archibald Wavell, was considerably outnumbered (the Italian army exceeded 200,000 in total while the British only had 30,000) he decided in December to throw everything he had at the Italians. This strategy worked and soon those who had not surrendered were in full retreat. By February, British forces had advanced 1700 miles and had taken half the Italian army prisoner. Mussolini's East African Empire of Somaliland, Eritrea and Abyssinia was also overrun in 1941 and here too over 100,000 prisoners were taken.

Equally humiliating for the Italian dictator was his failure to conquer Greece. Jealous of Hitler's success and upset at not being informed about the despatch of German troops to protect the Romanian oilfields, Mussolini launched an invasion of Greece in October 1940. However, his army was soon in trouble, the Greeks fought back and the Italians retreated. By the end of 1940 Hitler was forced to intervene in both the Balkans and Africa. He intervened in Greece not only to save Mussolini, but because he did not want the British to establish bases on his southern flank that might threaten the Romanian oil fields. On 6 April 1941 he launched simultaneous attacks on Yugoslavia, which capitulated in 10 days, and Greece, which was defeated in a month.

British troops had been taken out of North Africa and sent to Greece, but to little effect. They were evacuated to Crete, which Hitler took in May by means of a spectacular, but costly, airborne assault. Moreover, the troops taken out of Africa weakened the forces there at a time when a new German presence under Rommel was about to launch a counter attack. In March–April 1941 the British were pushed out of Libya back into Egypt. The ejection of a pro-German government in Iraq in May and the conquest of Vichy Syria in July could not compensate for what had been a succession of setbacks. A year after the fall of France the future looked no brighter, but then Hitler invaded Russia.

BENITO MUSSOLINI (1883–1945)

Mussolini was born in Predappio in the Romagna. He became a member of the Socialist Party and edited its newspaper *Avanti*. He served in the war and split with the Socialists over this issue. After the war in 1919 he founded the Fascist movement and became violently anti-socialist. He came to power in 1922 and gradually established himself as the dictator of a one-party-state. As he stated:

> This is our formula: all within the state, nothing outside the state, nothing against the state ... What occurred in October 1922 was not a change of Ministry, it was the creation of a new political regime.

from a speech of October 1925

His aim was to make Italy 'great, respected and feared' as he put it, and every Italian was to become a good Fascist:

> The whole country has to become a great school for perpetual political education which will make Italians into complete Fascists, new men changing their habits, their way of life, their mentality; their character and finally, their physical make-up. It will no longer be a question of grumbling against the sceptical, mandolin-playing Italians, but rather of creating a new kind of man who is tough, strong-willed, a fighter; a latter-day legionary of Caesar for whom nothing is impossible.

from a conversation in 1931

This theme of a link with the ancient Roman Empire was made manifest in Mussolini's expansionist foreign policy, with the take-over of Abyssinia (1935) and Albania (1939). He formed the Axis with Germany (1936) and aided Franco's forces in the Spanish

Civil War. At the most favourable moment in 1940 when he thought France was on the verge of collapse and the war was won, he entered World War Two, but met with disaster everywhere – in France, in Greece and in Egypt; he was no Caesar (he was called a 'Sawdust Caesar') and his soldiers were not heirs to the Roman legionaries. Although he had been popular at the time of the Lateran Accords with the Pope (1929), Abyssinia, and Munich (1938), he was discarded by the Italian people in 1943, following defeat in North Africa and the invasion of Sicily. He was rescued by the Germans and ruled a puppet republic in the north of Italy, but as the Allies closed in he was shot by Italian partisans on 28 April 1945 when trying to flee.

References

1. On one occasion a German plane carrying the relevant operational orders landed accidentally in Allied territory.
2. See especially Adam Adamthwaite, *Grandeur and Misery* (Arnold, 1995) and Robert J. Young, *France and the Origins of the Second World War* (Macmillan, 1996).
3. Churchill's speeches have been collected by R. Rhodes James; volume VI covers the period 1935–42.
4. See especially John Charmley, *Churchill: The End of Glory* (Hodder, 1993).
5. For a full discussion of Sea Lion see William Shirer, *The Rise and Fall of the Third Reich* (Secker and Warburg, 1960), Chapter 22.
6. See John Keegan, *The Second World War* (Hutchinson, 1989), p. 77.
7. On 24 August a German plane bombed London by mistake and the following day the RAF retaliated by bombing Berlin. There was little damage, but Goering was embarrassed and Hitler was furious; it has been suggested that these events also played a part in bringing about the switch of 7 September, though recent historical accounts dismiss this contention.
8. See A.W. Purdue, *The Second World War* (Macmillan, 1999), p. 61.
9. See A.P. Dobson, *US Wartime Aid to Britain* (St Martins, 1986).

Summary Diagram
The Second World War

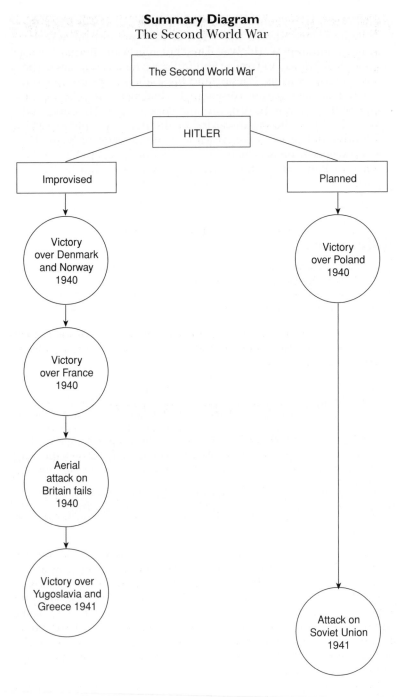

Working on Chapter 2

Note-making is the foundation of all your learning – the basis for both essay writing and revision. It is also an active process that requires you to concentrate while you read. The subdivisions of this chapter make it relatively easy to decide on headings, but deciding on the level of content is not so easy. Do not write out the whole book – there is no point – but on the other hand make sure you do not miss anything important. This is not an easy task at the beginning when you are unfamiliar with a topic.

The chapter is divided into two sections:

1) The Invasion of Poland
2) War in the West

The latter is subdivided into five further sections:

a) The Phoney War
b) The Scandinavian *Excursus*
c) The Fall of France
d) The Battle of Britain
e) Africa and the Balkans

Your main concerns will be to identify the main reasons for Hitler's phenomenal success in Poland and the west and, of course, why he failed to conquer Britain (see below).

Answering essay questions on Chapter 2

Consider the following questions:

1 'The military successes of Germany in 1939 and 1940 are explained more by the inadequacies and mistakes of its enemies than by German military superiority.' How far do you agree with this judgement? (*30 marks*)
2 'It was the strength and efficiency of the RAF which frustrated the German attempts to defeat Britain in 1940.' How far do you agree with this judgement? (*30 marks*)

You should use your introduction in your essay to address the question, define its terms where necessary and in effect answer it by explaining your view. The rest of the essay should then be used to justify the position you have taken at the beginning by developing the argument with relevant factual support. Remember that the greatest enemy of the effective essay is irrelevance: hence you should be addressing the question at all times, not necessarily always explicitly but certainly implicitly. By the time you reach your conclusion you should have the marks in the bag.

In these essays you are required to weigh up various factors in order to come to a judgement about the question. In each case you are being led by the question to consider one reason as most important. Thus it was Allied inadequacy rather than German military prowess that explains the defeats in May–June 1940 – and it was the skill of the RAF rather than the failings of the *Luftwaffe* that explains the outcome of the Battle of Britain. Of course you can either agree or disagree with the proposition, – provided you are able to back up the position you have taken; however, it is usually the case that complex events have complex explanations and a single explanation will not suffice. Thus in (1) you will have to give credit to German strategy as well as pointing out Allied inadequacies; and in (2) you could argue that Goering's strategic errors counted for more than the RAF.

These sorts of questions at A2 level are usually marked by a five-level mark scheme. Thus a **level one** response would be descriptive; a **level two** response would be analytical, but would be essentially a monocausal explanation and therefore unbalanced. **Level three** responses will see both sides of the coin, but will only deal with one side adequately; **level four** will be wide-ranging and will display a detailed understanding of the relevant causal factors, i.e. good analysis, a variety of explanations weighed and good factual support. The difference between level four and **level five** is likely to be the quality of the judgement. This candidate would, in the eyes of the examiner, distinguish him/herself by being in full command of the material and offering a convincing judgement with full confidence. In short, a candidate who really knows what he/she is talking about.

3 The Eastern Front 1941–4

POINTS TO CONSIDER

In this chapter you should consider why Hitler invaded Russia and why his initial successes were reversed. Could he have won or gained a negotiated settlement? You should also consider the social and economic impact of the war on the two countries involved, and appreciate how the Soviet Union recovered sufficiently to out-produce the Nazi regime.

KEY DATES

1941	22 June	Barbarossa: Hitler invades Russia
	19 July	Hitler switches troops from Army Group Centre
	5 December	Russian counter-offensive in front of Moscow
	11 December	Hitler declares war on the USA
1942	May	Unsuccessful Soviet offensive
	10 June	German offensive in south
	September	Paulus reaches Stalingrad; the battle begins
	November	Germans cut off in Stalingrad
1943	January	The *Wehrmacht* withdraws from the Caucasus
	31 Jan–2 Feb	The Germans surrender at Stalingrad
	February	Goebbels calls for Total War
	Feb–March	Manstein successfully counter-attacks
	July	Tank battle at Kursk: Soviet victory; Soviets go on the offensive
1944	27 January	Relief of Leningrad
	March	Soviet autumn and winter offensives lead to re-conquest of the Ukraine. Hitler occupies Hungary (19 March)
	April	Red Army enters Romania

1 The Decision

> **KEY ISSUE** When and why did Hitler decide to invade Russia?

There are a number of reasons that can be identified for Hitler's decision to invade Russia, but the problem is getting the balance right. There is of course the basic ideological reason: Hitler was fulfilling the mission he had clearly spelt out in *Mein Kampf* – the destruction of 'Jewish Bolshevism' and the creation of living space in Eastern Europe. In addition, there is the economic argument that Hitler resented Germany's dependence on Russia's raw materials; there is also the argument that by defeating Russia and depriving Britain of a potential ally the British would be forced to make peace; and further there is the growing concern that Germany had about Russia's expansionist aims, in particular with regard to Finland, Bulgaria and Romania, sources of raw material for the Reich. Hitler felt a clash was inevitable. Most historians see the ideological argument as paramount with the disputes over Eastern Europe determining the timing. However, some historians do not see Hitler as a man with a programme and point out that between June and November 1940 he hesitated and pondered the variety of options open to him. Of course his hesitation could be explained by his uncertainty about what Britain was going to do. As we have already stated, initially he expected the British to ask for peace and subsequently when they did not, he believed they could be bombed into submission. When this did not happen he took the decision to leave Britain undefeated and turn on Russia, believing (correctly) that Britain was not in a position to open a second front, and believing (incorrectly) that Russia would be quickly defeated. We should also not allow our post-war perception of the relative power of Britain and the Soviet Union to obscure the fact that in 1940 the British Empire was considered to be a far greater power than the USSR.

Already in the early phases of the campaign against France in May, Hitler's attention was turning to the east. On 30 June he stated that a 'demonstration of our military power' would overawe Britain 'and leave our rear free for the East'. On 21 July he ordered Brauchitsch, his commander-in-chief, to examine 'the Russian problem' and on the 31 July he informed his generals that the Soviet Union would be attacked in the spring of 1941. In August he sent officials to East Prussia to find suitable headquarters and in September he started transferring troops from the west to the east. However, there is no doubt that he did hesitate – he was completely foxed by Britain's failure (as he saw it) to make peace. What appears to have been decisive was Molotov's visit to Berlin in November 1940 during which the Soviet foreign minister outlined Russia's considerable territorial requirements. At that point Hitler decided that Soviet ambitions (conquest of Finland, annexation of more Romanian territory – Besserabia had been taken in June) were irreconcilable with Germany's interests (in particular the Reich's dependency on Romanian oil).

Accordingly, on 5 December 1940 he told his generals to attack Russia the following May and on 18 December he issued the official directive for the invasion, codenamed Barbarossa. There were objectors, but so many who had questioned Hitler's strategy previously had been silenced by his phenomenal success. The plan envisaged a rapid three-pronged attack aiming at Leningrad in the north, Moscow in the centre and Kiev in the south, surrounding Russian armies *en route.*

The ultimate objective was to acquire territory up to a line from the Volga to Archangel (see the map on page 35). The *Wehrmacht* felt they would need only 10 weeks (or 3 months at the most – no preparations were made for winter fighting) to achieve these objectives – and, most remarkably, the force to accomplish this massive task would be roughly the same size as that assembled for the attack on France in May 1940 (approximately 146 divisions, 3600 tanks and 2000 planes – fewer planes than against France, as many had been lost in the Battle of Britain). Hitler had no wish to fully mobilise the German economy and of course he had to leave large numbers to garrison the conquered territories in the west and in the Balkans. However, this was a serious underestimation of what was required – it was in fact a huge mistake. Why was it made?

First of all, it was believed that the Soviet Union was in bad shape. Hitler himself stated: 'you only have to kick in the door and the whole rotten structure will come crashing down'. Stalin had conducted purges against the officer corps in 1937 and 1938 depriving the Red Army of its best leaders and the poor Soviet performance against the Finns in the winter war of 1940–1 convinced military observers that the Russians would be a pushover. In addition, Germany had absolutely no reliable intelligence about Soviet strength at all – they had no agents, no spies. The Russians did only have about 150 divisions facing Germany, so that the armies were roughly equal in size; however, there were also 20 divisions on the Finnish border and a massive 133 divisions in the centre and the Far East. The Russians also had 20,000 tanks and over 8000 aircraft and although most of these were obsolete a small proportion were state of the art (1500 T-34 tanks for instance). The Germans also ignored the resources available to Russia east of the Urals. Clearly it could be argued that this campaign was doomed before it began – and yet, as we shall see, Hitler was so nearly successful.

An offensive was not practical until the spring and in the meantime diplomacy secured the allegiance of Finland, Hungary and Romania. Did Mussolini's disastrous adventures fatally change Hitler's timetable, as is sometimes claimed? Probably not – the delay from 15 May to 22 June was essential to take account of the exceptionally wet spring; and in any event, according to the *Wehrmacht*, it would be all over by September, before the autumn rains and long before the winter snow.

As for Stalin he retreated from his tough stance of November 1940 to a policy of appeasement in 1941. Another grain agreement was signed in January 1941 and the Soviets were scrupulous in fulfilling their part of the bargain. Stalin seems to have assumed that Hitler would not contemplate a war on two fronts. He ignored British warnings about the invasion believing them to be a ploy – but he ignored his own intelligence warnings too and many agents were executed after the war to cover up this fact. Stalin seems to have been genuinely surprised when Hitler attacked and this does seem rather odd. The British ambassador, Sir Stafford Cripps, described Stalin's frame of mind in 1941 as 'wishful thinking' and it does seem that he did not want to believe what everyone was telling him was going to happen.

2 Barbarossa (June–December 1941)

KEY ISSUE Why did Hitler fail to defeat the Russians in 1941?

The Germans achieved complete surprise when they attacked on 22 June. Army Group North drove towards Leningrad, Army Group Centre towards Moscow and Army Group South to Kiev. At first Barbarossa worked like clockwork: the Russians were cut up into sections and surrounded in pockets. Whole armies surrendered and cities fell as the Germans advanced over 400 miles in 3 weeks. Initially, Stalin's confidence was shattered by the invasion; he did not appear in public or speak to the nation until 3 July. However, once he recovered his nerve he was in absolute control; he ordered a scorched earth policy (that is to say everything in the Germans' path – crops, animals and so on – was destroyed so they could not be utilised by the enemy) and the formation of partisan groups, but above all he appealed to patriotism, calling on all Russians to defend Mother Russia against brutal foreign invasion.

Yet between June and August the bulk of the Red Army (in the west) was destroyed – this after all was a more important objective for the *Wehrmacht* than the acquisition of territory, since once the Soviet army was destroyed it was believed the whole state apparatus would collapse. Soviet losses in 1941 were in fact staggering – nearly 3 million men killed or captured, 15,000 tanks destroyed and over 8000 planes eliminated (over 1200 on the first day – most on the ground). This was a remarkable achievement by the *Wehrmacht* and a tribute to their skill and professionalism – though the Germans were aided by the paralysis of many Soviet generals who feared Stalin's disfavour if they withdrew. However, remarkable though the German achievement was, it was not enough.

Army Group Centre had achieved the greatest progress, but on 19 July Hitler decided to switch forces from it to the other army groups. Army Group South with its Hungarian and Romanian contingents had had a particularly difficult time and was making only slow progress. Whether or not this pause and change of plan saved Stalin is a moot point. Just as in France in the First World War, German objectives had not been reached – even at this early stage it could be argued that Barbarossa, like the Schlieffen Plan in 1914, had failed. Still, the pause in late July and August was necessary to enable the infantry to catch up[1] and secure areas already taken up, as well as to determine priorities. However, the very fact that decisions had to be made about priorities in itself shows that the initial victories had not been enough and that the German forces were stretched – the initial euphoria of the first few weeks gave way to a greater realism. The Germans just did not have the numbers. Indeed the infantry could not deal adequately with pockets of resistance, organise enormous numbers of prisoners and achieve effective occupation. At the same time the Germans were having equipment problems – German tank strength dropped by half in the first month – and the Russians were becoming increasingly determined and tenacious in defence (no doubt inspired by stories of the Germans' ruthless brutality in killing both civilians and surrendering soldiers). Hindsight suggest that the over-stretched Germans should probably have halted in September with Leningrad under siege and Kiev taken before the autumn rains, and waited until the spring, but now Hitler took the decision to take Moscow and the central offensive was resumed in October. This led to considerable panic in the Russian capital – millions left including the government, but Stalin stayed, having appointed Zhukov (see the Profile on page 42) to command the defence of the city. Thanks to an agent in Japan, Richard Sorge, who assured the government that the Japanese had their sights on the Pacific and not Russia, Stalin was able to denude his Far Eastern frontier and transfer men, tanks and airplanes from that theatre to Moscow. This infusion of fresh troops saved the day.

In any event, the German advance was slowed by the October rains, which turned the already poor Russian roads into liquid mud. Snow also began to fall in early November; there was a frost, and this enabled the advance to resume, though by this stage the German infantry divisions were down to 65% combat efficiency and the Panzers 35%. Even so, by the end of November the *Wehrmacht* was only 20 miles from Moscow with some advanced parties in the suburbs (legend has it some saw the sun glistening on the Kremlin domes). However, by the end of November extremely cold weather set in (−20°C) interfering with machinery (the Germans had no antifreeze!) and reducing mobility. The German soldiers did not have winter clothing and tales of fingers coming off with gloves and feet with boots are not apocryphal: at least 100,000 soldiers got frostbite and there were over 2000 amputations. By 5 December the German offensive had ground to a halt and on that day the Russians launched a counter offensive that succeeded in pushing the Germans back between 50 and 150 miles. Even before the attack on Moscow had been halted, the southern and northern fronts had come to a standstill and the south was already in retreat from Rostov.

On 8 December Hitler called a halt to all offensives. Already in November the German generals were planning for the spring and needed to make strategic withdrawals; however, on 16 December, Hitler, haunted by the spectre of the Napoleonic retreat from

Moscow, expressly forbade any withdrawal. This led to a series of rows in the High Command, which in turn led to a spate of resignations and dismissals including those of von Rundstedt, Bock, Guderian and even Brauchitsch. Having jettisoned his ablest generals, Hitler now took over as commander-in-chief himself. By the end of the year the situation was a stalemate but the Germans had lost over half a million men (over a million by February 1942 – 31% of the entire force[2]) and did not have any reserves. German conquests were vast, but the Russians were not defeated – Moscow, Leningrad and even Sebastopol in the south had not been taken, and the Russians still had 200 divisions. The Russians had shown immense courage and fighting spirit inspired no doubt by a sense of patriotism but also by a furious despair engendered by news of German atrocities. The Germans had missed the opportunity to come as liberators by conducting a politico-racial campaign of appalling brutality.[3]

How near did the Germans come to victory? Indeed, what constituted victory? Only perhaps in October did the Soviet state look vulnerable, thereafter it rallied and Stalin himself showed stoic fortitude, appearing in public for the Red Square parade on 7 November. Were the Germans defeated by the weather as is often suggested? This is a dubious argument since it ignores the fact that the *Wehrmacht* was supposed to have won by the end of September; in any event the Russian winter is no surprise – it comes every year and the conditions were the same for both sides (though the Russians were equipped for it). The truth is the Germans completely underestimated the Russians and never really had the numbers to achieve their goals. Barbarossa had failed and this failure was to be the second major turning point in the war. The third also came in December. On 7 December the Japanese attacked the US fleet at Pearl Harbour and a few days later Hitler declared war on the USA – with hindsight a baffling decision, but Hitler had an extremely low opinion of the Americans (and believed they would not fight as indeed did the Japanese).[4] So now it was a truly world war; however, it must be remembered that the majority of the fighting of the whole war took place on the Eastern Front – more people fought and died there than on all the other fronts around the globe put together. This was the end of *Blitzkrieg*, as in 1914 Germany now faced a war of attrition that it was ill equipped to win. The writing was on the wall.

JOSEPH STALIN (1879–1953)

Stalin, who was born Joseph Dzhugashvili in Georgia in 1879, trained to be a priest but became a Bolshevik instead. After the 1917 Revolution he rose to become the general secretary to the Central Committee (1922), from which position he was able to outmanoeuvre his opponents after Lenin's death (1924) and

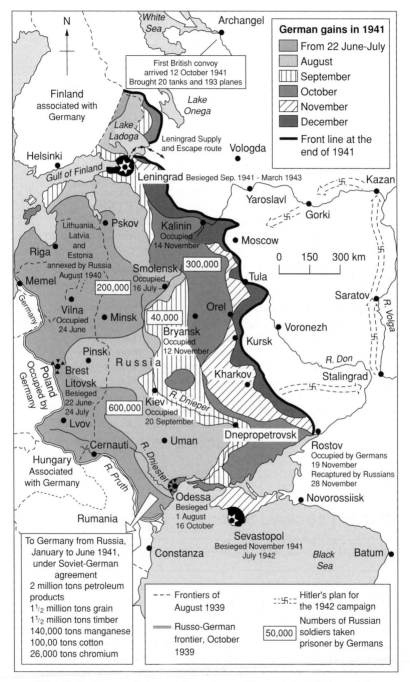

German gains in 1941

- From 22 June-July
- August
- September
- October
- November
- December
- Front line at the end of 1941

N

White Sea

Archangel

First British convoy arrived 12 October 1941
Brought 20 tanks and 193 planes

Finland
associated with
Germany

Lake Onega

Lake Ladoga

Leningrad Supply and Escape route

Vologda

Helsinki

Gulf of Finland

Leningrad Besieged Sep. 1941 - March 1943

Kazan

Yaroslavl

Gorki

Lithuania, Latvia and Estonia annexed by Russia August 1940

Pskov

Kalinin
Occupied
14 November

Moscow

Riga

0   150   300 km

Memel

Smolensk
Occupied
16 July

300,000

Tula

Saratov

R. Volga

200,000

Vilna
Occupied
24 June

Minsk

40,000

Orel

Voronezh

Germany

Bryansk
Occupied
12 November

Kursk

Pinsk

R u s s i a

Kharkov

Stalingrad

Brest
Litovsk
Besieged
22 June–
24 July

600,000

Kiev
Occupied
20 September

R. Dnieper

R. Don

Poland
Occupied by
Germany

Lvov

Cernauti

R. Dniester

Uman

Dnepropetrovsk

Rostov
Occupied by Germans
19 November
Recaptured by Russians
28 November

Hungary
Associated
with Germany

R. Pruth

Odessa
Besieged
1 August
16 October

Novorossiisk

Rumania

To Germany from Russia,
January to June 1941,
under Soviet-German
agreement
2 million tons petroleum
products
1½ million tons grain
1½ million tons timber
140,000 tons manganese
100,00 tons cotton
26,000 tons chromium

Constanza

Sevastopol
Besieged November 1941
July 1942

Black Sea

Batum

- - - Frontiers of
August 1939

═══ Russo-German
frontier, October
1939

Hitler's plan for
the 1942 campaign

Numbers of Russian
50,000 soldiers taken
prisoner by Germans

Map 4 Barbarossa (adapted from *Recent History Atlas, 1860 to 1960,*
M. Gilbert, Routledge, 1966, p. 71)

become sole leader. He coined the phrase 'socialism in one country' and attempted to make Russia self-sufficient by a series of Five Year Plans. He stated:

> We are fifty or a hundred years behind the advanced countries. We must make good this distance in ten years. Either we do it or they will crush us.
>
> *from a speech in 1931*

Stalin trusted no one and his paranoia led to mass executions and purges of both the party and the armed forces. His foreign policy was cautious and he surprised everyone by making a deal with Hitler in 1939, though he had little choice. He was true to the Pact and said at the time:

> The Soviet Government takes the pact very seriously. I can guarantee on my word of honour that the Soviet Union would not betray its partner.
>
> *Stalin to Ribbentrop 23 August 1939*

When Hitler turned on Stalin in 1941, the latter was momentarily stunned. He recovered, refused to contemplate peace and eventually fought back, defeating the Germans, enlarging the Soviet Union and spreading communism throughout Eastern Europe. From 1945 he consolidated his hold on his satellite states behind an 'iron curtain', thus helping to begin the Cold War. His paranoia contributed to its intensification.

Stalin was clearly one of Russia's most successful rulers but the kindly epithet 'Uncle Joe' belied his savage nature. When he became ill in 1953 his immediate entourage would not call a doctor as they feared another purge if he recovered. He died on 5 March of that year.

3 The Caucasus, Stalingrad and Kursk

KEY ISSUE How were the Russians able to turn the tide?

In January 1942 Stalin, buoyed by the successful defence of Moscow, ordered a somewhat over-ambitious winter offensive on all fronts, against Zhukov's advice. Although the Russians now outnumbered the Germans (by perhaps 4 million to 3 million) these assaults were too thinly spread and were unsuccessful. Undeterred Stalin approved a further offensive in the south in May. Hitler's plan for 1942 was also to concentrate on the south. Operation Blue, which had been discussed since November, envisaged a drive by Army Group South into the Caucasus to deprive Russia of her oil resources – though first the Crimea had to be taken. Halder, Hitler's Chief of Staff, got the impression that this was designed to lead to peace negotiations rather than the destruction of the Soviet state and it is significant that the Germans could only consider an offensive in one sector in 1942, clearly reflecting the limits of their resources.

In May, Marshal Timoshenko launched the Soviet offensive but it was a complete failure – not only did he fail to take Kharkov, but General Manstein was able to defeat two armies and take the Crimea as well. The Soviets lost half a million men killed, captured and surrounded in these campaigns. The German offensive proper, held up by the Soviet attacks, was launched in late June and initially enjoyed great success. Stalin had deceived himself into thinking that the main thrust would be in the centre against Moscow so once again he was taken by surprise. However, finally, from July, he was persuaded to allow his commanders to retreat, to prevent Soviet soldiers being surrounded and captured as they had been so many times before. This meant that the Germans were able to conquer vast tracts of territory as the Russians retreated – but took relatively few prisoners. In contrast to Stalin, who was now more amenable to advice, Hitler became more and more dogmatic, and less and less inclined to listen to others. In a bout of over-confidence brought about by initial successes he decided in July to conduct a series of operations simultaneously rather than in sequence. That is to say, he sent one army from Army Group South off to help against Leningrad, another to Stalingrad to secure the Volga and the other three into the Caucasus (he also transferred troops to Tunisia). This naturally reduced the effectiveness of the main thrust and by August the Caucasus advance began to slow as the army fanned out and its spearheads became smaller – neither Grozny nor the Caspian shore were reached let alone Baku – and Red Army resistance stiffened. The objective set for Operation Blue had not been met. Things were little better further north.

By September, General von Paulus's VIth army had reached Stalingrad, which was an important but not essential objective to protect the Caucasus flank. However, this battle developed exaggerated importance because of the significance attached to it by both Stalin and Hitler – for both leaders its capture became a matter of personal prestige. Throughout October and into November the Germans fought a vicious house-to-house fight[5] until, as winter closed in, about seven-eighths of the city was in their control. At this point the Soviets counter-attacked. Zhukov amassed a million men, 900 tanks and 1000 aircraft and attacked the Stalingrad salient from the north (where the allied Romanian, Hungarian and Italian armies crumbled) and south so that the city was surrounded and the German VIth army cut off. Hitler would not allow von Paulus to break out and withdraw. He became singularly intractable about this matter and placed his faith in the *Luftwaffe* – Goering stated he could supply the beleaguered army from the air (he could not). Von Manstein's relief army could only get as close as 40 miles to the city as the Germans were now outnumbered three to one in this sector. Renewed Soviet offensives threatened to cut off the German armies in the Caucasus. On 28 December Hitler finally agreed to withdraw from the Caucasus and 400,000 soldiers were expertly extricated from this potentially fatal situation – aided of course by the ongoing battle for Stalingrad.

By the end of January 1943, the German position in the ruined city had become impossible and von Paulus took the decision to surrender (despite his promotion to Field Marshal by Hitler). Over 100,000 Germans had died at Stalingrad and nearly that number surrendered, though only a few thousand would ever return to Germany. This was a highly significant victory. The legend of German invincibility was broken – it was the first surrender of a German army in the war – and it sent shock waves throughout the Reich. The military significance of this Soviet victory may have been exaggerated, but there is no doubting its enormous psychological effect on all Germans and especially on Hitler whose prestige was clearly undermined (though he sought to blame his allies for the disaster). After this event many Germans were plagued by pessimism about the war's outcome, and Hitler himself was no longer his old, ebullient self – the defeat left him an increasingly debilitated and shaken man.

Yet we must be careful not to read history backwards. The Russian victory was considerable but not decisive – it was a setback for the *Wehrmacht*, but it was far from finished, as Stalin soon discovered in early 1943. Buoyed by this victory Stalin once again overruled Zhukov and ordered a vigorous pursuit that over-stretched the Soviet advance. Manstein, despite being considerably outnumbered, counter-attacked in February and March and he even retook Kharkov. This rapid German recovery shocked Stalin and at this point he may have even contemplated peace negotiations based on the 1941 borders, but Hitler believed he could hold on to his conquests and planned another offensive.

What were Hitler's options? Clearly the great gamble had failed and most of the generals concluded that a largely defensive war was the only option. There could be no major offensive in 1943 though it was felt that another victorious battle might lead to a political solution. The offensive, code-named Operation Citadel, was designed to destroy the salient (a bulge in the line) at Kursk (see the map on page 40) in order to stabilise the front and consolidate the German hold on the conquered territory. It was originally planned for mid-April but, under pressure from some of his generals who wanted the new Tiger and Panther tanks, Hitler became hesitant and indecisive and kept on postponing the operation. His insistence on delay destroyed its chances of success since it gave the Russians time to build up their defences. Obviously any commander must weigh up the advantages of surprise against the benefits of preparation – but until 1943 Hitler backed surprise over preparation – his new-found caution was disastrous. By July when he finally ordered the attack, the Russians knew from their own and British intelligence when and where the blow would fall.

Many have seen Stalingrad as the great turning point in the war, but it was the great tank battle of Kursk that finally ended Hitler's hopes of holding on to the bulk of his conquests in Russia. Attacking from the north and the south, the Germans threw 700,000 troops and 2400 tanks into the salient, which was half the size of England, but they ran into a killing ground of carefully prepared defensive positions manned by over a million Soviet troops with about 3400 tanks. This, the greatest tank battle in history, was all over quite quickly as Hitler soon called it off (unnerved by Allied landings in Sicily) with the loss of half a million men. This was a shattering defeat for the *Wehrmacht*; after this the Germans lost the initiative. The Russians had always had superiority in numbers (prior to Kursk it is estimated the Red Army had 6 million troops to the *Wehrmacht*'s 3 million) but now they had superiority in tanks and in the air (they were out-producing the Germans) – while US trucks gave their troops speed and flexibility (the Germans were still very reliant on horses).

At the same time the Red Army launched offensives at Orel in the north and Kharkov in the south. The latter fell in August but Manstein was able to conduct a skilful retreat. At this point the Germans were still outside Leningrad, held White Russia in the centre and the Ukraine in the south. Hitler now realised that there had to be some strategic withdrawals and placed his faith in what he called an East Wall from Azov to the Baltic, but the Soviet autumn offensive soon made nonsense of this plan. Stalin's autumn offensive won back an enormous tract of land along 650 miles of front, up to 150 miles deep. On 6 November, Kiev was retaken and by the beginning of December, German forces in the Crimea were cut off.

By this time, Hitler's priority was the impending invasion in the west, which he reasoned he would first have to defeat before concentrating on the east – this front would now have to look after itself. However, at no time were the Germans given time to recover; the Red Army was not going to make the same mistake the *Wehrmacht* had made in the spring of 1943. So a winter offensive rapidly followed the autumn one, which resulted in the re-conquest of the Ukraine by March 1944. Winter efforts in the centre and north were less successful but the siege of Leningrad was finally lifted. By the spring of 1944, not only did Hitler lack the means to mount any offensive, but he did not have enough reserves to fight a defensive battle. Moreover, he was now faced with the threat of a seaborne invasion in France and an Allied breakthrough in Italy. He was also concerned about his allies' loyalty and so occupied Hungary in March. By April the Russians had entered Romania, crossed the pre-war Polish frontier and were at the Estonian border.

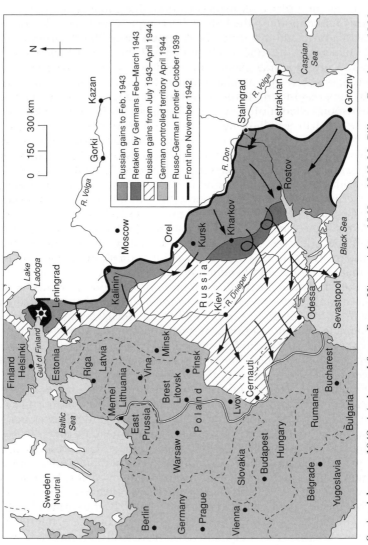

Map 5 Soviet Advances 1942–4 (adapted from *Recent History Atlas, 1860 to 1960*, M. Gilbert, Routledge, 1966, p. 81)

Russian gains to Feb. 1943
Retaken by Germans Feb–March 1943
Russian gains from July 1943–April 1944
German controlled territory April 1944
Russo-German Frontier October 1939
Front line November 1942

How do we account for the dramatic success of the Red Army in 1943? Quite clearly the key is logistical – Soviet superiority of numbers both in terms of soldiers and equipment proved decisive. In 1943, the Red Army was twice the size of the *Wehrmacht* on the Eastern Front and in some sectors the preponderance could be as high as 7 to 1. Of course Hitler had to disperse his forces – another 3 million were deployed around the rest of Europe and he had had to send 150,000 to North Africa. In addition, the Russians were able to make good their losses – increasingly the Germans were not able to do so – by October 1943 most infantry divisions were operating at only one-third of full strength. Indeed, the Russians had always had numerical superiority in personnel but they now had superiority in tanks and aircraft as well. Russian industrial production east of the Urals far exceeded that of Germany with its slave labour – in 1943 the Russians produced 30,000 armoured vehicles, the most the Germans ever achieved was 19,000 in 1944. By October 1943 the Germans only had 2400 tanks (of which 700 were fully operational) whereas the Red Army had 8400 and had taken delivery of over 100,000 US trucks – the Germans could only produce 82,000 in 1942 (and still relied on horses). Moreover, Russian tanks (especially the T34) and Russian planes were more than a match for their German equivalents. Similarly, as with the *Wehrmacht*, the *Luftwaffe* had to disperse its forces to deal with the RAF and USAF, whereas the Russian airforce was operating in a single theatre and could concentrate its forces.

Another important fact is that the Red Army had learnt from its previous mistakes and was now displaying increasing operational effectiveness – in addition to the immense courage and fighting spirit of the troops was added a mixture of timely retreats, in depth field defences and well-planned offensives with superior numbers: the Russians could concentrate their forces in a particular sector while much of the German army would be static on another part of the front. In addition Stalin provided inspired leadership and, although he was often over-ambitious and fired his generals with a frequency comparable to that of Hitler, he did at least listen to military advice and act upon it. In Zhukov he had an outstanding general. Hitler, on the other hand, was increasingly unwilling to listen to anyone. He had shown a certain military genius in attack but in defence he was a disaster: his static approach gave the Russians the initiative and his obsession with standing fast enabled the Red Army to destroy entire German armies – he always ordered withdrawal too late. Moreover he now had no one to blame but himself though he still contrived to blame others – in March 1944 he dismissed both Manstein and Kleist. Between the summer of 1943 and the spring of 1944, the Red Army had advanced as much as 600 miles in some places. There were German counterattacks and some German victories, but the pattern was one of continuous Russian offensives, leaving only brief periods when the front was static. The tide had turned.

GEORGI ZHUKOV (1896–1974)

-*Profile*-

Born of peasant parents, he worked in Moscow as an apprentice before being conscripted into the Tsar's army. In 1918 he joined the Red Army serving as a cavalry commander in the Civil War and later became an expert in armoured warfare. He was an able, popular commander, decisive, well organised, who paid close attention to detail and expected the utmost from his men. Stalin respected him, which perhaps explains why he survived the purges in the 1930s. In 1939 he commanded tanks in Mongolia and, as a general, became Chief of Staff in 1941.

In December 1941 he lifted the siege of Moscow, and in 1942 planned and executed the victory at Stalingrad. After being named Marshal of the Soviet Union in January 1943, he became Stalin's chief military adviser; subsequently he was involved in the planning or execution of almost every engagement in the war, including the counter offensives in 1943 and 1944. In April 1945 he personally commanded the final assault on Berlin and accepted the German surrender on 8–9 May on behalf of the Soviet Union. However, his immense popularity aroused the jealousy of Stalin who assigned him to a series of obscure regional commands after the war.

After Stalin's death in 1953 he returned to a central role in the Defence Ministry but fell out with Krushchev over his wish to make the army autonomous of the Communist Party (1957). Rehabilitated once again after the fall of Krushchev (1964) he was awarded the Order of Lenin in 1966 and allowed to publish his memoirs. He played a central role in Russia's victory; his ability to learn from mistakes and adapt to the German tactics, remain calm in the face of great adversity and retain the confidence of Stalin speak volumes for his ability.

4 The Economic and Social Effects of the War

KEY ISSUE What were the principal social and economic effects of the war on the Soviet Union and Germany?

a) Russia

What were the economic and social effects on the protagonists in this, the most important theatre of War? Firstly, it was a true test of the Soviet regime. In the first 6 months of the war most of the army had been lost as well as territory, which had contained one-third of grain production, 40% of the population and 60% of coal and steel production. However, the Soviet Union was in fact able to make a truly astonishing recovery thanks mainly to the highly centralised control that already existed and the truly heroic efforts of the people – the shift to a war economy required no essential change in Soviet economic practice. Immediately all males born between 1905 and 1918 were drafted but the most remarkable achievement was the relocation of industry beyond the Urals away from the German advance. Something like 1500 factories and 10 million workers were transported east in a spectacular and extraordinary, but largely improvised, effort. For example the Kharkov tanks works was turning out 734 tanks in the Urals just 10 weeks after the final evacuation of the factory in the Ukraine. This move, something akin to a second industrial revolution, built upon the fact that already, before the war, a substantial coal and steel industry existed beyond the Urals, which provided the USSR with about one-third of its production. This remarkable effort meant that already in 1942 arms production exceeded pre-war levels and more importantly exceeded that of the Germans as it had done in 1941 when much of European Russia was overrun. Moreover, Soviet production was able to keep well ahead of Germany even when the Third Reich stepped up production after 1942. This achievement was aided by the fact that the Russians, unlike the Germans, concentrated on only a small number of different types of weapon – two different types of tanks, five different types of aircraft, and so on – which were straightforward to manufacture and easy to maintain. Where production was deficient, as in trucks, food and steel, this to some extent was provided by the USA. Churchill had been quick to embrace the Russians as allies in June 1941 and although the Americans were not at war with Germany until December, they had already extended a generous Lend-Lease promise to the Soviet Union before that date. The British could do little to directly help, though bombing Germany and the campaign in North Africa did tie down significant German forces; however, US help proved to be very important even though it was played down by the Russians at the time and subsequently. Obviously the Russians had been able to stop the Germans, by themselves, but the speed of their recovery and subsequent advance owed a lot to Allied aid.

Soviet suffering was considerable in the occupied territory: 3 million prisoners and over a million civilians were eliminated in 1941 alone. So much land was lost that food production fell to a half of what it had been before the war and over a million people starved to death. In fact, the vast majority of Soviet citizens existed on the brink of starvation throughout the war. And yet exist they did – men, children and particularly women were drafted into agriculture, industry and the armed forces on an unprecedented scale – and provided three-quarters of the workforce on the land and half in industry. Working conditions were harsh, hours were long and rations were meagre; holidays were curtailed and housing conditions beyond the Urals were non-existent. However, the state did institute incentives such as bonuses and extra food rations to improve performance (Soviet society became more hierarchical as a result), but there were other factors that account for Russia's remarkable achievement:

i) Firstly, state control – the security apparatus of the Soviet state was important in maintaining national resolve through propaganda and fear – the labour camps were full and suspect minorities – such as Muslims in the Caucasus and the Volga Germans – were deported.

ii) Secondly, although there was collaboration, overall Nazi brutality – for the Germans this was a racial war to expel or eliminate slavs – was such that it left Russians with little choice but to support the devil they knew.

iii) Thirdly, and most importantly, there was an appeal to patriotism (though here we must distinguish Russia itself from the many republics). This was not a fight for socialist equality, but a Great Patriotic War for the preservation of Mother Russia. The spirit of patriotism was genuine but it was also to some extent artificially contrived – Russian heroes of the past such as Ivan the Terrible and Peter the Great were rehabilitated, decorations and orders which commemorated Tsarist generals were created, distinctions of dress and rank, abolished in the Revolution, were revived and even the Orthodox Church was enlisted to preach the crusade again the invaders (and as a result there was a remarkable religious revival). Vodka production was maintained (essential) and the arts were enlisted to sustain morale, though apart from Shostakovich's Leningrad Symphony little would have any lasting value.

However, Stalin was not going to rely on anything so subjective as patriotism. In December 1941 all workers in the war industry were placed under military law and could be shot if they failed to turn up. Holidays were suspended and the working day extended to 12 hours. Above all, the power of the party was enhanced – not initially when in fact its role was played down, but after the tide turned – so that by 1945 a quarter of the armed forces were party members – half the party. The Second World War was different from the First when Russia had collapsed, demoralised after $2\frac{1}{2}$ years of setbacks. In 1941–5 the great defeats had come at the beginning; after that there was resistance, hope and ultimately pride in pushing the enemy back. To some extent the Russians can be forgiven for thinking that they alone defeated the Nazis. After all, the war on the Eastern Front was fought with such ferocity that possibly more than 20 million Russians died.

b) Germany

Why were the Germans unable to match the Soviet effort, particularly when you consider the greater expertise of both their workforce and their military? First of all the Germans did not prepare for a lengthy war – they did not fully mobilise either their population or material resources. Why was this? The regime did not fully mobilise the economy, so the argument goes, for two reasons: one in order to maintain morale and, two, because *Blitzkrieg* did not require it. There is some debate about the former point – for some historians it is hard to believe that Hitler cared enough about his people to treat them with kid gloves.[6] For these historians poor economic performance was largely the result of inefficiency and the later increase in output due to force of circumstances. While the last two points have considerable validity, it does appear that Hitler had an acute concern for civilian morale and did not want to depress living standards – he wanted no stab in the back by disaffected civilians as had allegedly happened in 1918. Consequently the regime did not ask for sacrifices and a high level of consumer goods production continued well into the war. In fact, Germany did not fully mobilise its economy until 1942 and, when this did happen, it was largely due to necessity – the war had not been won quickly.

Germany's greatest economic weakness was the inefficiency of the state. Nazi Germany was run by competing authorities and characterised by the in-fighting of those with positions of responsibility. Hitler himself was no planner or organiser and seems to have thrived on 'divide and rule' tactics. A change only came with the realisation that Germany's situation was becoming serious. Prior to 1942, Goering presided over the chaos – however, with the appointment of first Todt (who was killed in a plane crash) and then Albert Speer, a 37-year-old amoral technocrat, as Minister of Munitions in February 1942, things began to change. Speer rationalised and streamlined the economy; he created a Central Planning Board and held regular meetings with the big industrialists to ensure production priorities. He was able to double war production by mid-1943 and more than treble it by mid-1944. Priority was given to the mass production of new weapons. Older men (60–65) and women (17–45) were mobilised for war from January 1943 – though in practice the number of women employed did not really rise. Despite Nazi ideology, which maintained a woman's place was in the home, 51% were in the workforce prior to the outbreak of war and this did not change much; however, women were never truly applied to war work as such, as they were in Britain and the Soviet Union. In 1944 a full range of price controls and rationing was introduced though up to that point the German civilian had been cushioned by the plundering of the occupied territories (which came to provide one-third of many foodstuffs) and the use of conscripted labour. To a large extent this was slave labour. By 1944 over 7 million foreigners were working in Germany – wretchedly housed, poorly fed and constantly mistreated – though on a scale determined according to racial category (so Frenchmen would be treated better than, say, Russians who were treated appallingly).[7] Ironically Germany achieved its highest levels of production in the last 6 months of 1944, by which time it was too late. In any event a glance at the table at the end of this chapter shows that in relative terms Germany could not really compete with its opponents.

For one thing the German population at 76 million was just too small. By 1944, the average age in the *Wehrmacht* was $31\frac{1}{2}$, 6 years older than the average GI. As we have already indicated, the mobilisation of women was to some extent limited by ideology, and slave labour itself was just not really efficient. In addition, Germany lacked key natural resources – rubber, iron ore and oil – and although synthetic substitutes were pioneered, its synthetic oil industry was targeted by the bombers and almost came to a standstill in September 1944 (despite the building of underground facilities). Another problem was the interdependence of the German economy – thus aircraft production reached its peak in the autumn of 1944 when there was insufficient fuel for the planes. Similarly coal was being produced in sufficient quantities, but unable to be transported because of the destruction of the railways – and once Silesia and Lorraine were overrun the steel industry ceased to be. Towards the end of the war other sectors of the economy collapsed with equal or greater suddenness in a chain reaction.

What is also surprising, given their technical expertise and good education system, is the Germans' failure to build on their technical lead of 1939 and create new weapons – all they tended to do was upgrade existing equipment though this of course very much fits in with the short war philosophy. But even subsequently there was insufficient focus on a few tried and tested items. To take the aircraft industry as an example, there were in fact too many different projects – 425 different models were on the books, most of which turned out to be costly failures. Moreover, when an excellent jet fighter plane was developed – the Messerschmitt 262 – Hitler intervened to make it carry bombs and render it ineffectual. Similarly, the Germans had 151 different types of lorry and 150 different types of motorcycle. Ironically the nation that pioneered missiles and jet aircraft was being defended by a horse-drawn army.

Morale was good early on because Germany appeared to be winning. The apprehension of 1939 gave way to euphoria in 1940 and 1941, though hereafter some apprehension returned. There was some disquiet in the winter of 1941–2, but Stalingrad was the real turning point. However, the regime had built up such a reservoir of goodwill by its triumphant early successes – not only the successes of the war but the achievement of full employment and the reversal of many aspects of Versailles in the 1930s – that the vast majority remained loyal to the bitter end. Although he disappeared from public view from 1943, Hitler retained considerable personal support and for many the spell was not broken until perhaps the end of 1944 or even later with Allied occupation. There was some criticism – it was joked as early as 1943 that Hitler had retired to write a book called 'My Mistake' – but there were no mass uprisings, no mutinies. Although the Nazi state was a police state, oppression alone cannot account for the tremendous war effort and popular loyalty. Resistance movements were few and inconsequential – a coup was the only possibility, but the July 1944 bomb plot (an attempt by disaffected officers to blow Hitler up – see page 91) not only failed, it was greeted with widespread horror – not just among the ordinary people, but in the military too when it was seen as an act of treason.

As Hitler faded from the limelight his place was taken by Josef Goebbels, the diminutive propaganda minister. In February 1943, he called on the populous to make greater sacrifices and prepare for Total War. It is difficult to measure the effect of his propaganda but clearly there had developed a discrepancy in 1942 between optimistic reports and the reality of setbacks. However, once the desperate nature of the situation was accepted and acknowledged, Goebbels was successful in calling for resistance. Many felt they were fighting a war for racial survival and as fear of the approaching 'slavic hordes' increased, people became resigned to their fate: 'better enjoy the war; the peace will be terrible' was a common remark.

Between June and September 1944 so much occupied territory was lost that the German economy began to falter. Few were convinced by the promise of 'wonder weapons' and the reality of looming defeat could no longer be avoided. The German people were to experience both fear and apathy in equal measure – though for many, devotion and hope never died; many continued to support the regime right up until the time the Allied armies appeared. The question about the effect of bombing on civilian morale is a difficult one to evaluate, but clearly in the last 6 months of the war when Germany's air defences were negligible, it must have done a great deal to destroy people's will to carry on – it certainly disrupted the economy. For the vast majority survival became the main concern. As Michael Burleigh has put it, 'what followed is a story of progressive isolation of a leadership determined to go down in flames from an increasingly atomised civilian and military mass increasingly bent on personal survival. The latter literally lost faith, and had to confront a terrible inner emptiness'.[8] In the last 6 months of the war the Nazi state literally fell apart, but no one overthrew the *Führer* and many fought to the last, though whether or not the Allied call for unconditional surrender was a factor in this decision is rather a moot point.

Table 3 Wartime Aircraft Production Figures

State	1939	1940	1941	1942	1943	1944	1945
USA	5856	12804	26277	47836	85898	98318	49761
USSR	10382	10565	15735	25436	34900	40300	20900
UK*	8190	16149	22694	28247	30963	31036	14145
Germany	8295	10247	11776	15409	24807	39807	7540
Italy	1800	1800	2400	2400	1600	–	–
Japan	4467	4768	5088	8861	16693	28180	11066

*Includes the commonwealth.

Table 4 Tank Production Figures, 1940–4

State	1940	1941	1942	1943	1944
Germany	2200	4800	9300	19800	27300
USSR	2700	6500	24400	24000	28900
USA	400	4200	23800	29400	17500
UK	1400	4800	8600	7400	5000

Table 5 Population and Steel Output

Country	Population in 1939	Steel output in tons (highest figure in the 1930s)
UK	47,961,000	13,192,000
France	41,600,000	6,221,000
USSR	190,000,000	18,800,000
USA	132,122,000	51,381,000
Germany	76,000,000	23,329,000
Italy	44,223,000	2,323,000
Japan	71,400,000	5,811,000

Table 6 Maximum Mobilisation Strengths

UK	5,000,000
India	2,150,000
USA	11,700,000
USSR	11,500,000*
France	5,000,000
Germany	9,500,000†
Italy	4,000,000
Japan	4,000,000

* At least 6,000,000 more served before becoming casualties.
† At least 4,000,000 more served before becoming casualties.

Superior resources won the war – the victors had greater numbers of people and made more weapons. A glance at the tables should make it patently obvious that, provided they had the will to fight to the end, the Allies could not lose. Some of the most obvious points that can immediately be drawn from these figures is that the population of the Soviet Union was approximately the same as that of Germany, Italy and Japan put together. Moreover, as early as 1942, in its first year of war, the United States out-produced the combined Axis powers in terms of aircraft, guns and tanks, and it is clear that throughout the conflict the Soviet Union always out-produced the Germans, even when the latter had achieved their peak of production in 1944. Similarly, the Axis Powers were only able to mobilise about 21 million fighting men in World War Two whereas the Allies mobilised over 40 million. It is hard to see how the Germans could have won after 1941, though Richard Overy has reminded us that Allied victory was far from inevitable.[9] There is another side to this argument. By 1942, almost the entire resources of continental Europe were in German hands and Japan had wiped out the western colonial presence in Asia – and industrial strength is just one factor – fighting ability, the skill of the leaders, politics and morality all have to be taken into account (see Chapter 7).

References

1. The infantry only covered about 20 miles a day whereas the motorised divisions could easily cover 50.
2. See William Shirer, *The Rise and Fall of the Third Reich* (Secker and Warburg, 1960), p. 1039.
3. This brutality was not just the work of the SS; the *Wehrmacht* was very much involved too – despite postwar protestations of innocence.
4. Shirer, p. 1069.
5. In house-to-house fighting the Germans lost their advantage of superior skill and organisation.
6. For example see R.A.C. Parker, *The Struggle for Survival* (OUP, 1989), p. 136.
7. Speer literally got away with murder by escaping the noose at Nuremberg in a feat worthy of Houdini. His protestations of ignorance and remorse still take in historians, e.g. Max Hastings in the TV programme, *The Nazis in Colour*, but for a balanced view, see the new biography by Joachim C. Fest, *Speer: The Final Verdict* (Weidenfeld and Nicholson, 2002).
8. Michael Burleigh, *The Third Reich: a New History* (Pan, 2001), p. 758.
9. Richard Overy, *Why the Allies Won* (Jonathan Cape, 1995).

Summary Diagram

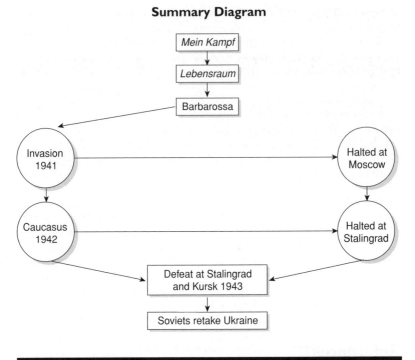

Working on Chapter 3

Notemaking

The headings of this chapter are as follows (with some indication of what is important therein):

1) The Decision – reasons for the invasion and its timing
2) Barbarossa – why did the invasion not succeed?
3) The Caucasus, Stalingrad and Kursk – when and why did the turning point occur?
4) The Economic and Social Effects of the War
   a) Russia – how did Russia survive and revive?
   b) Germany – why did the Germans fail and yet fight to the end?

Answering an essay question on Chapter 3

I German success against Russia in the initial phase (1941–2) was largely due to Soviet incompetence. How far do you agree with this judgement?

This question leads the candidate on by suggesting an answer, but as ever you have to be careful to consider alternative possibilities. A balance has to be struck between German tactics, German mistakes, the scale of the endeavour, as well as the Russian response.

4 The Tide Turns in the West 1942–4

POINTS TO CONSIDER

In this chapter you will see how the Western Allies were able to defeat the Germans in North Africa, knock Italy out of the war, eliminate the U-boat menace and overcome the *Luftwaffe*. You should also consider how important these developments were in relation to the Soviet effort and how significant they were in paving the way for an Allied cross-channel invasion of France and the opening of the real second front.

KEY DATES

1941	June	Hitler attacks Russia
	December	Hitler declares war on the USA
1942	January	Rommel on the offensive
	April-June	Peak of U-boat success
	July	First Battle of El Alamein; Rommel halted
	August	Monty halts Rommel at Alam Halfa
	October	Second Battle of El Alamein; Afrika Korps defeated
	November	US forces land in North Africa
1943	January	Roosevelt and Churchill meet at Casablanca
	April/May	Tide turns in U-boat war
	May	Germans surrender in Tunisia
	July	Allied invasion of Sicily; Mussolini falls. Hamburg devastated.
	September	Italy switches sides
	Nov/Dec	Big Three meet at Teheran
1944	January	Anzio landing
	Feb/Mar	*Luftwaffe* decisively defeated

1 The Desert Campaign

> **KEY ISSUE** How was Rommel defeated?

To recap: a year after the fall of France, Britain had had precious little success in stemming the Axis tide. Churchill's decision to withdraw troops from North Africa to Greece may well have prevented victory in Libya – it had certainly allowed the Germans to get established there, and it certainly did not prevent the Nazi takeover of Greece. However, the German attack on Russia had taken the pressure off and, adopting the policy that 'my enemy's enemy is my friend', Churchill was quick to embrace Stalin. In the Soviet Union Britain at last had a substantial ally. But of even more significance for Britain perhaps was the adhesion of the USA to the Allied cause in December – in particular, Roosevelt's decision to give priority to the defeat of Hitler over Japan's Hirohito.

When the Grand Alliance came into being in 1941, the war in Africa was for Britain practically the whole war – but for the Russians and Americans it was a sideshow. It was certainly small scale compared to the Eastern Front, but it turned out to be of crucial strategic importance. It was a campaign of great fluidity, of movement fought over great distance in which the balance of advantage swung back and forth – and although the forces were relatively small, their supply proved to be difficult and often determined the outcome. The heat and the sand proved problematic for both soldiers and equipment alike.

In the spring of 1941, British forces had been thrown back 370 miles; however, the front stabilised, and by November Auchinleck was in position to launch an offensive.[1] In a confused campaign Rommel's Afrika Korps was pushed back 340 miles to El Agheila but once his forces were replenished, he was, by the beginning of 1942, ready to launch a counter-offensive. Whereas British deployment – static positions that could be bypassed and cut off – was poor, Rommel's approach was characterised by flexibility, speed, improvisation, quick thinking, daring and even recklessness. In January and February of 1942 he pushed the British forces back to Benghazi and only called a halt because the Italians wanted to concentrate on taking Malta. However, after the experience of Crete, Hitler was not keen on any invasion and chose to bombard the island into submission;[2] he therefore sanctioned a renewal of Rommel's offensive in May. This was a dramatic success and pushed the British back 570 miles into Egypt as far as El Alamein, a 45-mile strip of territory between the Qattara Depression and the sea that could not be outflanked. It looked as though he would go on to take Alexandria and the whole of Egypt, but by that stage his forces were much reduced and his supply lines overlong. Rommel always gambled, but he was usually saved by the unimaginative response of the British commanders. Hitler was delighted with his success, promoted him to Field Marshal and envisaged the Afrika Korps driving through the Middle East and linking up with his armies of the Caucasus, marching south – a scenario also envisaged by the worried Allies.[3]

Churchill on the other hand was humiliated – he was in Washington when he heard of the fall of Tobruk in June. Coming on top of the fall of Singapore in February this was a difficult time for the British Prime Minister – though he easily survived a vote of censure in the House of Commons in July. Still, he badly needed a victory – for his own political future as well as for Britain's standing in the eyes of the Russians and Americans. The collapse of the British position in North Africa negated any possibility of the Western Allies opening up a second front in Europe in 1942 – an option already tenuous because of Japanese victories and U-boat successes – and reinforced by the failure of the raid on Dieppe in August. Now the Americans decided to rush 300 Sherman tanks to the 8th Army in North Africa and land their own 1st Army in French North Africa (Operation Torch) to threaten Rommel's rear.

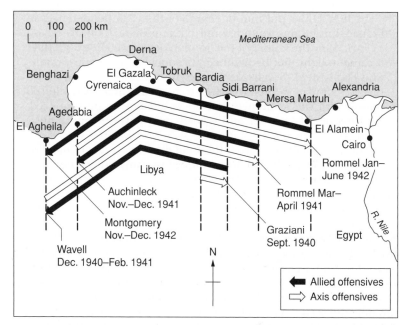

Map 6 The Desert Campaign 1940–2 [adapted from *The Second World War: An Illustrated History*, A.J.P. Taylor (ed.), Penguin, 1976, p. 156]

ERWIN ROMMEL (1891–1944)

-Profile-

Educated at Tübingen, he distinguished himself in World War I and became an instructor at the Dresden Military Academy thereafter. Later he commanded Hitler's headquarters guard 1938–9 and led a Panzer division in the invasion of France in 1940. He displayed such drive and initiative that he was subsequently put in charge of the Afrika Korps.

His success in North Africa earned him the sobriquet 'the Desert Fox', the Field Marshal's baton and the admiration of his opponents. However, he was kept short of equipment and was overwhelmed at the battle of El Alamein in November 1942. He was withdrawn from North Africa on the grounds of ill-health in March 1943 just prior to the collapse of that front.

In 1944 Hitler put him in charge of the Channel defences in France, but he was wounded during an air attack on his car on 17 July. After the failure of the bomb plot against Hitler (20 July) it came to light that he had been in touch with the conspirators who had wished to make him head of state. Hitler did not want such a popular soldier to stand trial, so Rommel was offered poison with the assurance that he would not be dishonoured. He died on 14 October and was later buried with full military honours.

During his military career Rommel displayed exceptional gifts of initiative and improvisation and he remains one of the best-known generals of World War Two.

In fact the balance was already changing – it needed to because Rommel was a superior general, and he also possessed superior weaponry, both in terms of his panzer tanks and his anti-tank guns. In July, at what is sometimes called the First Battle of El Alamein, Auchinleck had fought Rommel to a standstill. However, Churchill did not appreciate the significance of this success and flew to Cairo to dismiss him. He was replaced by General Alexander and at operational level (after the death of General Gott in an air crash) by General Bernard Montgomery. 'Monty' as he was known inherited Auchinleck's plans and with typical self-confidence (and self promotion) claimed them as his own. Immediately in August he was able to halt Rommel's attack at Alam Halfa. By now the British 8th Army had considerable superiority over the Afrika Korps in terms of men and tanks;[4] however, Montgomery would not be rushed into an offensive – he wanted to restore morale, put an end to the mentality of retreat, and ensure that, when the battle came, the enemy would be destroyed and be unable to recover again. He wanted to put an end to the see-saw campaigning that had characterised this theatre for over 2 years.

By the time he attacked in October, he had 195,000 men to the enemy's 103,000 and he had 1300 tanks to Rommel's 500.[5] He should have won and did – but it was not easy and casualties were high. Still, Montgomery was prepared to take casualties and this second Battle of El Alamein proved to be decisive. Much of the enemy force was destroyed (more of it would have been had Rommel obeyed Hitler and not withdrawn) and it was sent into a headlong 1500-mile retreat

BERNARD MONTGOMERY (1887–1976)

- *Profile* -

The son of a bishop, Montgomery was educated at Sandhurst and served in the First World War. In 1940 he commanded a division that was evacuated from Dunkirk and in the following year he was given the command of the 8th Army in North Africa. He quickly restored confidence and the will to win and launched the battle of El Alamein in October. Adopting Alexander's strategic plans and enjoying overwhelming odds he was able to achieve a bloody victory and, after a series of hard-fought engagements, he was able to push the Afrika Korps back to Tunis. This success and his high visibility made Monty highly popular with the British public.

His subsequent rather pedestrian efforts in Sicily and southern Italy were something of an anti-climax, but his appointment as the commander of ground forces for the Normandy invasion of 1944 put him back in the thick of military activity once again. Here his strategy was characterised by caution, meticulous preparation and unflagging tenacity as he engaged the bulk of German forces thereby enabling the Americans to break out (i.e. open up another flank – see the map on page 92). He subsequently liberated Brussels, but his uncharacteristically ambitious attempt to turn the German flank by taking Arnhem went disastrously wrong. Later he took much of the credit for halting Hitler's last offensive through the Ardennes (the 'Bulge') in December 1944–January 1945 and then went on to invade northern Germany where he took the surrender of the German forces of Holland, Denmark and northern Germany in May.

After the war he was made a Viscount, became Chief of the Imperial General Staff (1946–8) and deputy commander of the North Atlantic Treaty Organisation (NATO – 1951–8). He published his Memoirs in 1958. A controversial figure, Monty earned the devotion of his soldiers and the detestation of his colleagues in equal measure. A difficult man with a large ego, he did not get on well with his American colleagues, Eisenhower in particular – with whom he had a fundamental strategic disagreement over the invasion of Germany. When Montgomery's memoirs were published, Eisenhower, who was then President, was so incensed that he suspended current business and called his former colleagues to Camp David to discuss it! Montgomery's military reputation remains mixed, but by 1942 Britain needed a success and he provided it.

across Libya. Tobruk was taken on the 13th November and Benghazi on the 20th. By early 1943, Rommel was forced to retreat to Tunisia.

Simultaneously an Anglo-American force under General Dwight D. Eisenhower landed in French Morocco and Algeria in November 1942, to close the net around the Afrika Korps. Thanks to the tact of Eisenhower, Anglo-American cooperation worked remarkably well though the position of the Vichy French authorities was a complex one. In the end, French Morocco and Algeria declared for the Allies (this prompted Hitler to occupy the whole of Vichy France in November) but French Tunisia did not. Surprisingly – especially given the tenuous position of the German VIth army in Stalingrad at this time – Hitler decided to pour troops into Tunisia (150,000 in number) and prolonged the campaign by 6 months. This in turn precluded any Allied landing in the west in 1943, though at Casablanca in January of that year Roosevelt and Churchill decided to invade Sicily.[6]

DWIGHT EISENHOWER (1890–1969)

-Profile-

Born in Texas, Eisenhower graduated from West Point in 1915 and by 1939 was the chief military assistant to General MacArthur in the Philippines. In 1942 he assumed command of Allied forces for the invasion of French North Africa. Despite his lack of experience he soon learned to translate theory into practice and exhibited a rare genius for smoothly coordinating the activities of interallied staff – possibly his most valuable contribution to the war effort given the difficult nature of some of his commanders like Patton and Montgomery. His success in North Africa and the preponderance of US forces in the planned invasion force led to his appointment as Supreme Commander. Despite poor weather he resolutely launched the invasion of France, which became an enormous success. His preference for a broad front strategy and his decision to halt forces at the Elbe so as not to upset the Russians subsequently drew a great deal of criticism, but he may well have been right on both counts.

After the war he was awarded many honours including an honorary OM (the British Order of Merit) and in 1950 he was made supreme commander of the newly established NATO. However, in 1952 his popularity led to his nomination by the Republican Party and subsequent election as the 34th President of the United States; he was re-elected in 1956. His sincerity, integrity and flair for conciliation marked him out as the ideal man to conduct the military operations of the Grand Alliance, to smooth over differences and hold it together.

Eventually, the Axis forces in Tunisia were pushed back and forced to surrender because they ran out of supplies. Though the combined German and Italian forces may have outnumbered those of the Allies by May 1943 when they did give up, fully three quarters of their supplies were not getting through and the Afrika Korps was reduced to distilling alcohol for fuel. No plans were made for evacuation (though Rommel was flown home), consequently the Allies took somewhere between 150,000 and 250,000 prisoners (historians cannot seem to agree on a figure) – the largest number of Axis prisoners taken to date. Clearly the Allies had now seized the initiative in this theatre and if the defeat had been a humiliation for Hitler, it was a disaster for Mussolini.[7] His days were numbered.

2 The Invasion of Italy

KEY ISSUE To what extent did the Italian campaign fail to fulfil the hopes the Allies placed in it?

It was agreed by the British and American leaders at Casablanca in January 1943 that after the fall of Tunisia an invasion of Sicily (Operation Husky) should be launched to ensure control of the Mediterranean; however, no decision was taken on what should happen to Italy thereafter. The British, Churchill in particular, developed a Mediterranean strategy that envisaged not only the invasion of Italy, but landings in the Balkans too. It was argued that such action would draw German forces away from France and give the cross channel invasion a much greater chance of success. The Americans disagreed; they argued that everything should be concentrated at the decisive point – further commitment of forces in the Mediterranean would divert essential men and material away from the French landing. Given this disagreement, the future strategy after Husky was left open-ended. The final decision was in fact left to Eisenhower.

Allied forces landed on Sicily in July and the Germans (and Italians) were taken completely by surprise. Deceived by the 'man who never was' – a dead body with bogus plans placed in the sea off

Spain – the expectation was that the assault would come elsewhere, in Sardinia. Although the Allied invasion of Sicily was ultimately a success (the island was overrun in just over a month) the operation was badly planned and poorly executed. The Allied soldiers fought well, but the Allied commanders hardly covered themselves in glory – the enemy was pushed back rather than defeated and allowed to escape to the mainland. Montgomery and Patton did not get on, though fortunately personal differences at the top did not affect good relations at lower levels.

The most important outcome of the conquest of Sicily was the fall of Mussolini on 25 July. Since 1940, he had given the Italian people nothing but war, humiliation and defeat, and after his removal by the King, support for fascism simply evaporated. Here now was an opportunity to knock Italy out of the war; Mussolini's removal made an invasion both attractive and practicable. In any event, Eisenhower had already decided to go ahead with an invasion, convinced that the capture of the southern Italian airfields at Foggia would bring more of Germany and German-controlled industry within range of Allied bombers.

Unfortunately Italy did not turn out to be the 'soft underbelly of Europe' as Churchill had predicted. The Germans moved swiftly to occupy most of the peninsula and given the mountainous terrain, numerous river valleys and their fierce resistance, the campaign soon ground to a halt. Even prior to Mussolini's fall, Hitler had made plans to take account of the possibility of Italian defection. Although Badoglio (who took over from Mussolini) assured the Germans of his loyalty he was not believed and, while he played a double game, the Germans rushed troops to Italy so that by September they had control over most of northern and central Italy and were able to move swiftly to seize Italian occupied territory in France and the Balkans.[8]

The Germans were right to mistrust Badoglio; soon after he took over, he opened secret negotiations with the Allies, but faced with the demand for unconditional surrender and the threat of a German takeover, he dithered for weeks. In the end, Italian surrender occurred at the same time as the Allied invasion at the beginning of September, but little was done to prevent the German take-over. Even Mussolini, under arrest since July, was not guarded properly: he was 'rescued' in a daring raid and set up as a puppet ruler of the 'Italian Social Republic' based in small towns around Lake Garda in the north. However, he ceased to be of any significance – the Germans now ran Italy.

Although Rommel had felt that all forces south of Rome should be withdrawn, Field Marshal Albert Kesselring, who commanded Rome and the south, had different ideas. Aided by Montgomery's rather sedate progress, he decided to form a line along the Volturno, 30 miles north of Naples where he was able to conduct a brilliant defensive campaign against unimaginative opponents. Naples was 'liberated' on 1 October and the Allies hoped to be in Rome by the end of the month; in the event Rome was not taken until June 1944. The Allies were only able to advance 70 miles in 8 months as the Germans carried out retreat by stages to a naturally strong defensive belt, the Gustav Line, which incorporated the dominating mountain heights of Monte Cassino; here the Allies were held up from January to May 1944.

In the heady days of October 1943 when everything was going well, Churchill had started to plan a Balkan campaign. He seemed to prefer this theatre, where the British were ostensibly in charge and seemed to favour a postponement of the cross-channel invasion (Overlord). He may have even hoped that a second front in France might not have been necessary. However, the Americans saw the Italian campaign as a sideshow and when the 'Big Three' (Roosevelt, Churchill and Stalin) met at Tehran (28 November–1 December 1943), Stalin disappointed the British by insisting that Overlord should be carried out at the earliest opportunity. Italy was secondary to the Russians, though they favoured a landing in the south of France (to be code named Operation Anvil). Churchill was prepared to give up his Balkan strategy in return for US commitment to a continued offensive in Italy. However, by the end of the year the campaign had become bogged down and it was decided to outflank the Gustav Line by making a landing at Anzio. This occurred in January 1944, but the US commander failed to take the initiative and was soon bottled up on the beach-head by swift German action. The breakthrough did not come until May, but once again the Germans were allowed to get away as General Mark Clark was more interested in being the liberator of Rome than destroying the *Wehrmacht*. After Rome, Churchill wished to make a rapid advance north, but he eventually conceded that troops should be diverted to the landing in the south of France (Anvil had been renamed Dragoon). This operation has often been criticised as pointless, but this overlooks the value of the port of Marseille.[9]

The Italian campaign has not had a good press either, but there is no doubt that it removed troops from France and tied down substantial German forces that could have otherwise been used elsewhere. The Germans placed about 35 divisions in Italy, leaving roughly 61 in France; of course these numbers are dwarfed by the approximately 190 divisions in Russia, but it must be remembered that most of the divisions on the Eastern Front were below strength. Indeed it has been calculated that the divisions in the west consisted of something like 2.44 million men whereas those on the Eastern Front were only 2.85 million in number.[10] In terms of diverting German resources, the Italian campaign can be viewed as a success; in terms of allowing an invasion of central Europe from the south, it was clearly a disappointment.

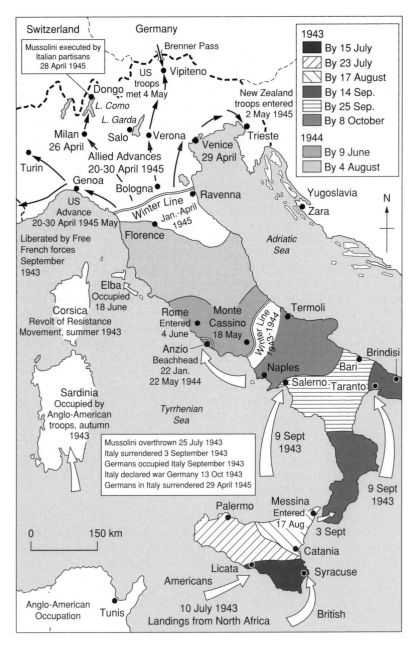

Switzerland

Germany

Mussolini executed by
Italian partisans
28 April 1945

Brenner Pass

US
troops
met 4 May

Vipiteno

New Zealand
troops entered
2 May 1945

Dongo

L. Como

L. Garda

Salo

Verona

Venice
29 April

Trieste

Milan
26 April

Allied Advances
20-30 April 1945

Turin

Genoa

Bologna

Ravenna

Yugoslavia

Zara

N

US
Advance
20-30 April 1945 May

Winter Line
Jan.-April
1945

Liberated by Free
French forces
September
1943

Florence

Adriatic
Sea

Elba
Occupied
18 June

Corsica
Revolt of Resistance
Movement, summer 1943

Rome
Entered
4 June

Monte
Cassino
18 May

Winter Line
1943-1944

Termoli

Anzio
Beachhead
22 Jan.
22 May 1944

Naples

Salerno

Brindisi

Bari

Taranto

Sardinia
Occupied by
Anglo-American
troops, autumn
1943

Tyrrhenian
Sea

Mussolini overthrown 25 July 1943
Italy surrendered 3 September 1943
Germans occupied Italy September 1943
Italy declared war Germany 13 Oct 1943
Germans in Italy surrendered 29 April 1945

9 Sept
1943

9 Sept
1943

Messina
Entered
17 Aug

3 Sept

Palermo

0   150 km

Catania

Licata

Americans

Syracuse

Anglo-American
Occupation

Tunis

10 July 1943
Landings from North Africa

British

1943
■ By 15 July
▨ By 23 July
□ By 17 August
▨ By 14 Sep.
☰ By 25 Sep.
▧ By 8 October
1944
▨ By 9 June
□ By 4 August

Map 7 The Invasion of Italy 1943 (adapted from *Recent History Atlas,
1860 to 1960*, M. Gilbert, Routledge, 1966, p. 79)

3 The Battle of the Atlantic

KEY ISSUE How were the Allies able to defeat the U-boat?

Operation Husky was not the only matter decided at Casablanca in January 1943: priority was to be given to the defeat of the U-boat, for without control of the Atlantic the opening of a second front in France would be impossible, and without a second front Hitler might not be defeated. The crucial importance of this campaign should not be underestimated.

Prior to the war Hitler had given little thought to the navy, and at its outbreak the surface fleet was really quite tiny consisting of only three battleships and eight cruisers. Moreover, with the scuttling of the *Graf Spee* in 1939 and the sinking of the *Bismarck* in 1941, German naval prestige had suffered an irretrievable blow; the surface ships were removed from the Atlantic, confined to Norwegian waters and the Baltic, and even threatened with decommission by Hitler himself! The U-boat (*unterseeboot*) fleet was also small; however, whereas capital ships took a great deal of time and money to construct, submarines could be produced quite quickly. Indeed the expansion of the U-boat fleet and a submarine strategy was the only viable option open to the German Naval High Command. Moreover, as it became clear in late 1941 that the war was not going to be won quickly, it became the responsibility of the German navy to keep Britain and the USA at arm's length so the *Wehrmacht* could concentrate on finishing off the Soviet Union. This strategy even offered the possibility of British defeat. Great Britain depended upon overseas supplies for food, raw materials and military equipment. German submarines were so effective at sinking Allied shipping and starving Britain of essential supplies that the U-boat nearly succeeded where the *Luftwaffe* had failed. British imports of dry cargo in 1938 had been running at about 68 million tons; by 1940 this was down to 44.2; by 1941 31.5 and by 1942 22.9. This was an alarming trend. No wonder Churchill stated, once victory came, that 'the only thing that really frightened me during the war was the U-boat peril'.[11] Britain adapted to reduced imports by cutting rations, growing more at home and simply deleting some foods – but if British defeat could just be avoided, the U-boats could also prevent German defeat. There was nothing the huge US army could do to help defeat the Third Reich if it could not be brought to Europe and supplied there. Britain alone was not strong enough to open up a second front. The only way the Western Allies could beat Germany was by winning the Battle of the Atlantic (the term was coined by Churchill in March 1941).

The man in charge of the U-boats, Grand Admiral Karl Dönitz, had long seen the potential for submarine warfare, but Raeder, his superior, had favoured the construction of a surface fleet and U-boat development had been neglected. Doenitz calculated that he needed 300 U-boats to bring Britain to her knees, and had he had that number in 1940 he may well have done so. In fact he only had about 20 operational ocean-going vessels. The conquest of Norway, Holland, Belgium and France opened up all sorts of possibilities for U-boat deployment but Hitler did not give U-boat production any sort of priority until July 1940. The initial aim then was to sever Britain's vital maritime links and bring her to her knees. Despite the small numbers, Dönitz very nearly did this.

Initially, U-boats operated individually and were able to pick off ships sailing independently. In the period July to October 1940, 144 unescorted ships were sent to the bottom and 73 in convoy with the loss of only two U-boats. As convoys became more common the U-boats concentrated into 'wolf-packs' to give them strength in numbers. The vessels would be dispersed on a patrol line across the convoy route in groups of three and once contact with a convoy had been made, radio contact would be made with other vessels and about 15 would converge and attack under cover of darkness. In October 1940, 20 out of 34 ships in a convoy were lost by this tactic. The Allies countered by improving the range of escorts for the convoys, so that by 1941 continuous protection could be provided on the western approaches, from Iceland and from Newfoundland. More heavily escorted convoys were not such easy prey and in March 1941 it cost the Germans five U-boats to sink 19 ships. However, the initial Allied tactic was simply to use intelligence to locate and avoid the U-boats rather than destroy them and by the end of 1941, Britain was to some extent able to contain the threat, though Hitler had ordered many to the Mediterranean to protect supplies to Rommel's Afrika Corps. However, up to this point, shipping losses had exceeded replacements by nearly 7 million tons, so the battle was not being won.

KARL DÖNITZ (1891–1980) — *Profile*-

Born near Berlin, he entered the navy as a cadet in 1910 and served on the cruiser *Breslau* until joining the submarine service in 1916. He bitterly resented Germany's defeat, became a staunch advocate of submarine warfare and, after Hitler came to power, he secretly supervised the creation of a new U-boat fleet, becoming its commander in 1936. In January 1943 he succeeded Admiral Raeder as commander in chief of the navy, but during the course of this year the U-boats were to suffer a permanent defeat. Among those sailors lost was Dönitz son, Peter. He placed his faith in the development of new, advanced submarines and for this purpose Hitler agreed to hold the Baltic ports at all costs; however, too few were ready by the time the war ended – in 1943 the admiral had expected the war to go on into 1946 and 1947, but this proved to be wildly optimistic. By the winter of 1944–5 when the end looked more imminent Dönitz actually planned to send submarines, plans, engineers and officers to Japan to sustain their war effort though little came of this.

His loyalty and ability won him the complete confidence of Hitler who appointed him as his successor at the end of April 1945. In office for only about a week, he unsuccessfully tried to sign a separate peace with the west, before agreeing to unconditional surrender on 7 May. He was subsequently arrested and sentenced to 10 years' imprisonment at Nuremberg in 1946. As late as 1953 while still in jail he continued to insist that he was Germany's legal head-of-state! On his release in 1956 he remained an unreconstructed Nazi. His memoirs appeared in 1958.

At the end of 1941, the whole situation changed: Hitler declared war on the United States and Dönitz immediately transferred the weight of his effort to the US coast where the U-boat commanders enjoyed a second 'happy time' sinking unescorted US vessels lit up by the lights on the shoreline (and sometimes lit up by their own lights). During February 1942, 65 ships were sunk; 86 in March; 69 in April; and a high of 111 in May. Finally, the Americans instituted a convoy system. The U-boats moved south to the Gulf of Mexico and the Caribbean. June saw 121 ships sunk, but by the end of that month this area was included in the convoy system and the U-boat commanders switched to the 'Black Gap' in the mid-Atlantic where air escort was still almost non-existent. A glance at the table indicates that the U-boats were able to keep up a devastating level of destruction. By now, Dönitz had over 100 U-boats in service (now refuelled at sea by 'milch cows'[12]) with another 250 under construction. 1942 was a good year for the German submarines: they were the main obstacle to the USA bringing its power to bear in the European theatre and had played an important part in postponing the Allied invasion of France in 1943. Dönitz could look forward to 1943 with optimism – with even greater numbers available to him he might even be able to prevent an invasion in 1944.

Table 7 Maximum Mobilisation Strengths

Date	Total merchant shipping losses (tons) (approx.)
September–December 1939	425,000
January–March 1940	250,000
April–June 1940	450,000
July–September 1940	870,000
October–December 1940	860,000
January–March 1941	900,000
April–June 1941	1,100,000
July–September 1941	410,000
October–December 1941	450,000
January–March 1942	1,350,000
April–June 1942	1,750,000
July–September 1942	1,500,000
October–December 1942	1,650,000
January–March 1943	1,200,000
April–January 1943	660,000
July–September 1943	450,000
October–December 1943	230,000
January–March 1944	340,000
April–June 1944	125,000
July–September 1944	190,000
Oct–Dec 1944	120,000
Jan–Mar 1944	190,000
April 1945	75,000

The atrocious weather conditions in the winter of 1942–3 led to a reduction in the number of sinkings but the U-boats hit back in March. In one incident about 40 U-boats took on over 90 vessels and sank about 22 for the loss of only one. Indeed a total of 108 ships were sunk in March, which must have made Dönitz believe victory was within his grasp. Remarkably though, he was about to suffer a sudden, dramatic and almost complete defeat as the Allies went on the offensive. In May between 30 and 40 U-boats were sunk (Dönitz's son was among the victims) forcing the Admiral to withdraw them from the north to the south Atlantic; however, a further 54 were lost in June and July, and another 119 went to the bottom between September 1943 and May 1944. Between June and December 1943, 141 submarines were lost and only 57 ships sunk.

The U-boat menace had been eliminated in just a couple of months. How had this happened? The answer is complex, but it was really a case of everything coming together at the right moment. It has been suggested that the outcome of the Battle of the Atlantic mainly depended on code-breaking,[13] but when the end came it was brought about more by tactics and technical innovations than intelligence.

Of course intelligence did play an important part. British ability to crack the enigma codes (see page 79) played a decisive role in enabling the admiralty to locate the U-boats and re-route the convoys throughout 1941. But when in 1942 the Germans added a fourth wheel to the enigma machine this rendered it indecipherable until the end of the year – at which point the British discovered that the Germans had been deciphering Royal Navy codes all along; consequently these were changed in 1943. So, the Allies had something of an intelligence blackout in 1942, which was reversed in 1943 – a reversal that also mirrors the fortunes of the two navies.

Basically by May 1943, the convoys were now protected by all the latest technical innovations: long range Liberator aircraft with short wave radar and searchlights to pick out the U-boats on the surface at night; small aircraft carrier escorts to give the convoys protection from the air when the Liberators were out of range or unavailable;[14] support groups of destroyers whose purpose was to hunt down and destroy U-boats; and a remarkable device, the high frequency direction finder, HF/DF, or 'Huff Duff' as it was colloquially known, which picked up the short wave radio messages between the U-boats. Often the first message a U-boat sent would be its last. Remarkably the Germans never caught on to this device. Of course all of these technical and tactical advances should not in any way allow us to forget the courage and skill displayed by the seaman of both the navy and merchant marines; their contribution was fundamental

Although Dönitz may have been optimistic about 1943, in truth he was losing the war of attrition before May. U-boat losses were steadily rising, but the decisive factor was the dramatic increase in US shipbuilding production that meant that by 1943 more ships were being built (and manned) than were being lost. The time for a German victory had passed. Dönitz knew he had been beaten when he went to see Hitler at the beginning of June 1943, but he now placed his faith in technical innovations and new types of submarine. However, fortunately for the Allies these developments took place too late. The type VII had been superseded by the longer range type IX in 1942 and the development of a schnorkel in 1944 enabled the vessels to avoid surfacing;[15] however, the revolutionary type XXI, which was three times as fast underwater and would no doubt have given the Allies a real headache, was only ready in 1945 by which time the war was lost. The U-boats continued to take a hammering – so much so that fully 75% of the men who served in them died.[16]

Whereas the Allies had constantly innovated in order to beat the U-boat, the Germans only belatedly began to innovate in response to the defeat in May 1943 – though credit should go to the bombers, which delayed the new submarine building programme. The U-boat campaign therefore ultimately failed to bring Britain to her knees and failed to prevent the arrival of men and materiel from the USA. It was a victory in many ways as important as the Battle of Britain, but one that has never really captured popular imagination. Moreover, it was a victory that paved the way for final victory.

4 Strategic Bombing

KEY ISSUE How effective was strategic bombing?

The role of strategic bombing is a little less clear cut. The word 'strategic' in this context is used to distinguish this sort of bombing from tactical bombing in support of the army or navy and covers a myriad of meanings from the bombing of specific industrial targets to the blanket bombing of cities in order to terrorise the civilian population. Although most of the war in Europe revolved around land warfare, few other aspects of the conflict have proved as historically controversial as strategic bombing. Prior to the war, there was an exaggerated fear of the power of the bomber; from Baldwin's statement that 'the bomber will always get through' to the horrific destruction of Guernica in the Spanish Civil War, people were convinced that civilian casualties in war would be colossal – the British government anticipated 600,000 deaths in the first 2 months, whereas Britain's total for the entire war was 60,000 – and many were convinced that bombing might render land campaigns superfluous and might even win the war on its own. However, the experience of the *Luftwaffe* over Britain in 1940 seemed to indicate that prewar assumptions were false; daylight bombing led to too many losses and night bombing proved to be too inaccurate. Similarly, the RAF's bombing campaign over Germany in 1940 and 1941 did not work either, though the conclusion drawn was that this was because there were insufficient aircraft. It was certainly true to say that before the war, Britain had concentrated on fighter production for defence and had too few bombers to make any impact at the outset. Accordingly, a decision was taken in the summer of 1941 to massively expand bomber command. The RAF hoped for 4000 bombers by 1943; but, in practice, it never had more than about 2000 operational.

The key advocate of the bombing campaign was Sir Arthur 'Bomber' Harris who was appointed Commander-in-Chief of Bomber Command at the beginning of 1942, though it is also true to say that Churchill, Roosevelt and the USAAF were all keen proponents of this policy. From the British point of view, bombing was initially the only way to strike back and there were no qualms about hitting civilian targets – after all the *Luftwaffe* had bombed British civilians and revenge was an important element in the policy's *raison d'être* (main reason) – in short it was good for morale. It was also a way of assisting the Soviet

Union; when Churchill met Stalin in August 1942 to rebut Soviet criticism about Britain not pulling her weight, he maintained the British
could 'pay our way by bombing Germany'. Stalin was enthusiastic in
response.

RAF bomber losses in 1940 and 1941 had been quite considerable
(492 and 1034, respectively) so night bombing was adopted to avoid
losses, but unfortunately it also avoided the target. Therefore, industrial targets were ruled out and heavy bombing of cities to destroy
civilian morale was really the only option open to the RAF. In 1942,
this was considerably expanded and Air Chief Marshal Harris sent out
three spectacular 1000 bomber raids. These were good for publicity,
but overall the results were disappointing – the targets were often
not found, and if found the bombing was often inaccurate with the
consequence that damage was minimal. Still these raids had put
the *Luftwaffe* on the defensive, and at Casablanca in January
1943 Roosevelt and Churchill reaffirmed the Allied commitment to
strategic bombing – to soften up the enemy and assist a ground
invasion.[17] It was also agreed that the RAF and USAAF would conduct
a combined bomber offensive though in truth this term disguised a
deep difference of opinion – the operations would in fact be separate:
the US airforce would bomb industrial targets and communications
by day, the RAF would hit the cities by night. Basically the Americans
disapproved of the British tactics of bombing civilians, but then they
had never been bombed. From the British point of view, Bomber
Command still represented a degree of independence of action and
to some extent, for this reason, any change of policy was resisted.

The campaign in 1943 was disappointing and by the end of the
year the losses were becoming unacceptable. The main problem was
that the bombers were operating beyond the range of fighter escorts,
and were too vulnerable to the German fighter planes. Losses for the
USAAF by the autumn reached such a high level (20%) that daylight
bombing operations had to be postponed. Meanwhile the RAF concentrated on the same targets over and over again – the Ruhr
(March–June), Hamburg (July, August) and Berlin (from August);
however, civilian morale was not broken, despite some spectacular
results, particularly in Hamburg where 40,000 died in a horrendous
firestorm: on 27 July thousands of incendiary devices set off fires that
reached over 1000°C in the city centre; this in turn created a firestorm
of up to 150 mph which sucked in both people and, more importantly, oxygen. Lack of oxygen in fact suffocated the occupants of shelters before the fire cremated them. The police president of Hamburg
described the anguish:

> amidst the howling of the fire-storm, the cries and groans of the dying,
> and the constant crash of bombs ... children were torn away from their
> parents' hands by the force of the hurricane and hurled into the fire.
> People who thought they had escaped fell down, overcome by the

devouring force of the heat and died in an instant. Refugees had to make their way over the dead and dying. The sick and infirm had to be left behind by rescuers as they themselves were in danger of burning ... No flight of imagination will ever succeed in measuring and describing the gruesome scenes of horror in the many buried air-raid shelters. Posterity can only bow its head in honour of the fate of these innocents, sacrificed by the murderous lust of a sadistic enemy.[18]

Hamburg, however, was an exception brought about by accurate bombing and particular weather conditions. A similar raid on Nuremberg the following March only resulted in 129 deaths for the loss 500 crew. Air Marshall Harris's claims that the RAF would bring Germany to her knees were not being fulfilled. Indeed despite the death, destruction, and disruption, people were soon back at work and German industrial production continued to rise into 1944. However, here too the tide was about to turn, and the key was the P-51B Mustang, an American fighter plane.

Basically the bombers needed to be convoyed and once the Mustang was given the requisite range with the simple addition of bigger fuel tanks, this situation was transformed overnight. In fact, the Mustang played as import a role in 1944 as the Spitfire had in 1940; it took on the *Luftwaffe* and won. In February 1944, the Germans lost 450 fighters; they lost another 450 the following month and they never recovered. Although the production of planes was maintained, the Germans did not have sufficient pilots to replace those lost. This was a dramatic turning point. The true nature of this victory was disguised by the fact that in the spring and summer of 1944 the Allied airforces were redirected to France to assist in the D-Day invasion (by, among other things, destroying the French railway system to severely restrict the movement of the *Wehrmacht*). One measure of the extent of the *Luftwaffe's* defeat is the fact that at the time of the invasion in June 1944, German aircraft were counted in their hundreds whereas the Allies had in excess of 10,000. The British and Americans now had total air superiority.

Once the *Luftwaffe* was defeated, daylight bombing of specific targets became practicable. In the autumn and winter of 1944–5, US attacks on the synthetic oil industry led to serious shortages, so that production was reduced to a trickle. Similarly the RAF attacked the steel industry in the Ruhr and in the second half of 1944 production there fell by 80%. By the winter of 1944–5, Germany was carved up into isolated economic regions living off accumulated stocks, and while bombing did not entirely break morale, people did become apathetic and selfish – absenteeism became widespread. Precision bombing in the last year of the war did finally undermine Germany's capacity to continue the war.

The Germans tried to hit back with terror weapons, the pilot-less bomb, the V-1[19] and the unstoppable rocket, the V-2, but production difficulties (created by Allied bombing raids) meant that insufficient numbers were produced (9300 and 1115, respectively) and in any event they were far from accurate. The Germans also pioneered jet aircraft (the ME163 *Komet* and ME262), but as with the advanced U-boats it was a case of too few too late (see the next chapter).

So, what is the verdict? Was strategic bombing morally correct? Was it effective? In answer to the first question, Churchill quoted Moses 8:7: 'now those who sow the wind are reaping the whirlwind' and this seems a reasonable repost to critics. Of course the destruction of Dresden in February 1945 where over 50,000 died may, with hindsight, seem gratuitous, but at the time it seemed justified by its assistance to the Russians in creating confusion in civilian evacuation and hampering reinforcements.

Was it effective? 100,000 airmen died killing somewhere between 500,000 and a million Germans. However, civilian morale was not broken (until society fell apart) and may have even stiffened resolve by bringing people together in a shared danger. However, bombing Italy seemed to work where industrial production was reduced by 60% and ultimately industrial production was reduced in Germany too. An investigation by the US government concluded that German production was reduced by 9% in 1943 and 17 in 1944, though Albert Speer the Nazi Minister for Armaments put the figure at more like 40%. Moreover, bombing created a widespread diversion of resources – the *Luftwaffe* was taken away from the Eastern Front in 1943, and by 1944 something like 2 million people were taken up with anti-aircraft defence. In the last year of the war, when precision bombing became practicable, the oil and steel industry came to a standstill. In fact in the last 9 months of the war, German economic life was paralysed. However, because the success of the bombers coincided with the collapse of the *Wehrmacht*, it remains a difficult subject to assess.

Was strategic bombing a 'misapplication of resources' (Purdue) or 'decisive' (Overy)? Bombing did not defeat the enemy, but it made a significant contribution to the Allied victory – especially in the final stages. Moreover by 1944 it had led to the elimination of the *Luftwaffe* as a credible force; this had not necessarily been the campaign's principal aim, but it was a highly significant by-product. However, 'Bomber' Harris was denied the peerage given to all other major British commanders and his aircrew were denied a distinctive medal of their own. This seemed to reflect the feeling that with strategic bombing the British had somehow descended to the level of the enemy. On the other hand, it can always be argued 'the end justifies the means.'[20]

So, in the Mediterranean, at sea, and in the air, the tide had decisively turned in the years 1943–4. Hitler's days were numbered – the liberation of Europe was at hand, and not before time, for this was a truly evil regime.

References

1. By this stage the British had 700 tanks as opposed to the enemy's 400.
2. Malta did not succumb and the island was awarded the George Cross.
3. Mussolini even went to North Africa and picked a white horse for the victory parade in Cairo.
4. Rommel's supplies were being intercepted and there was no prospect of reinforcement.
5. Rommel was absent, ill in Germany with stomach cramps – was this psychosomatic?
6. The Allies also demanded the unconditional surrender of the Axis powers.
7. He had been urging a peace with Stalin to concentrate on this theatre.
8. The subject of the novel and film *Captain Correlli's Mandolin* by Louis de Bernières (Secker and Warburg, 1994).
9. See especially R.A.C. Parker, *The Struggle for Survival* (OUP, 1989), p. 192.
10. Ibid. pp. 191 and 193.
11. Quoted in Richard Overy, *Why the Allies Won* (Jonathan Cape, 1995), p. 48.
12. Submarines that simply contained fuel.
13. See Parker, p. 54.
14. In 1943 149 out of 237 U-boats destroyed were sunk by aircraft – either long-range or from carriers.
15. It should be remembered that contrary to cinematic portrayal the U-boats operated mainly on the surface.
16. Of 1162 built, 941 were sunk or surrendered. When the war ended 49 were at sea and 47 surrendered (the other two went to Argentina).
17. Unlike Harris neither thought it could, by itself, win the war.
18. Quoted in R.A.C. Parker, *The Struggle for Survival* (OUP, 1989), p. 156.
19. V = *vergeltingswaffen* – revenge weapon.
20. The saying is usually ascribed to the seventeenth-century German theologian, Herman Busembaum.

Summary Diagram

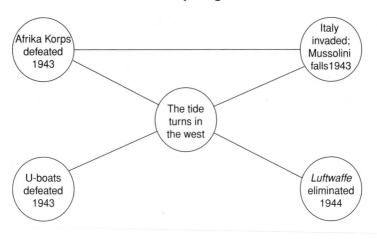

Answering essay questions on Chapter 4

1. 'The U-boat menace was mainly defeated by superior technology'. How far do you agree with this judgement?
2. 'The Allied strategic bombing offensive made no significant contribution to the defeat of Nazi Germany.' How far do you agree with this judgement?

As far as Question 1 is concerned you may feel you can largely agree with the statement, but do not forget you have to consider all the factors that account for the defeat of the U-boats – and of course it is not just a case of Allied efforts but German mistakes too (e.g. failure to develop new submarines fast enough, etc). Question 2 is much more difficult because although it requires you to undertake a full discussion of strategic bombing, the topic is allied to the whole question of Nazi defeat and this would also require you to make mention of some of the other (more important?) factors that account for German defeat.

The examiners will be looking for a balanced answer that goes a little beyond the topic of strategic bombing; however, it is likely that an essay that focuses as much as 90% on the bombing could still do very well.

5 Behind the Lines

POINTS TO CONSIDER

In this chapter, which deals with a number of different topics, you should consider the extent of collaboration in occupied Europe, the timing of decisions about the holocaust, the reasons for the Allied edge in technology and intelligence, and the strength of the Grand Alliance.

KEY DATES

1939	**January**	Hitler predicts the destruction of the Jews
	October	Nazi euthanasia programme begins
1940	**October**	Destroyers for bases deal
1941	**March**	Lend-Lease Bill
	June	*Einsatzgruppen* follow the *Wehrmacht* into Russia
	August	The Atlantic Charter signed
	September	Russian POWs gassed at Auschwitz
	December	USA at war
1942	**January**	Wannsee Conference
	May	Destruction of Lidice
	August	Churchill visits Stalin
	December	Vichy France occupied
1943	**January**	Churchill and Roosevelt meet in Casablanca
	April	Katyn Massacre revealed
	August	Danish government removed
	November	Big Three meet in Teheran
1944	**June**	First launch of the VI
	July	Destruction of Oradour-sur-Glane
	August	Warsaw Rising
	October	First launch of the V2; Churchill and Stalin make percentage agreement.
	November	Himmler orders the destruction of the death camps
1945	**February**	Big Three meet at Yalta

1 Nazi Europe

> **KEY ISSUE** What was the balance between collaboration and resistance in occupied Europe?

Until late 1943 German occupation enjoyed large-scale acquiescence; after all it was felt by many to be a permanent state. However, those fascists and Catholic conservatives who believed for a while that Hitler's New Order would usher in an era of European cooperation to protect European culture from Anglo-American influence were to be disappointed. Hitler's main priority was to win the war, not reorder Europe, though his guiding principle was racial. Thus certain Nordic peoples – Scandinavian, Dutch and Flemish – were considered acceptable but the rest were not. In the east, Hitler had a vision that entailed German colonisation and mass deportation,[1] but military security and exploitation were as important as racial domination until the war was won.

German control was something of a patchwork and very little territory was actually annexed (that was planned for after the war). Power ultimately rested with Nazi Governors, be they civilian or military. There were military governors in France, Belgium, Serbia and Greece for strategic reasons. In other areas there were civilian governors, though what remained of Poland had a Governor General; Bohemia and Moravia (today the Czech Republic) were a protectorate and the Baltic and Russia were placed under a Reich Minister. Half of France was ruled by its own (Vichy) government though the Germans occupied the whole of France at the end of 1942; similarly Denmark had its own government until August 1943 when it too was occupied. Bulgaria, Rumania, Hungary, Slovakia and Italy were allies, though all of these bar Bulgaria were occupied as the Allies closed in.

The Nazis clearly lacked the personnel to run such huge areas so they tended to rule through the existing structure of authority; famous collaborators like Quisling in Norway were the exception rather than the rule. In general the Germans were not all that enthusiastic about local Nazis and realised that government would have to have some credibility with the local populous if German interests were to be served.

Economic exploitation initially consisted of looting, but subsequently the occupied territories came to compensate for the German labour shortage. As we have already indicated, by 1944 there were about 7 million foreign workers in the Reich the majority of whom were Russians (nearly 3 million), Poles and French (in each case over a million). The East Europeans were virtual slave labourers and were worked to death. Indeed there was little scope for collaboration in the east, where racial and political ideology precluded any form of cooperation. There was therefore a missed opportunity in places like the Ukraine where initially the Germans had been welcomed as liberators.

The vast majority of people in occupied Europe had little to hope for but survival, and therefore passive collaboration was really the only option. Initially there was quite a bit of economic dislocation with both employment and transportation curtailed. Many lost their jobs and there was widespread poverty. In these circumstances it is understandable that the majority put their survival and that of their families before anything else – particularly in the early stages when a German victory seem inevitable. Of course for obvious reasons, something of a veil has been drawn across the extent of collaboration in occupied Europe though there is clearly a difference between active and passive collaboration. Active collaborators have been portrayed as a small and unrepresentative group – once the war was over this portrayal served to salvage national respect in order to achieve reconciliation and reconstruction. However, it also served to obscure the reality of Hitler's Europe. Obviously it was only a minority who were active collaborators, but it would be wrong to assume that most Europeans were in the resistance. After all 150,000 non-Germans joined the SS! Vichy France in particular was quite eager to collaborate and in many cases anticipated German policies, rounding up undesirables and transporting Jews. As we have already indicated, Hitler missed an opportunity for greater cooperation by ignoring those who were willing to cooperate in the creation of a New European Order; Hitler allowed his racial bias (against the French, for instance) to get in the way of any practical political considerations.

German rule was primarily undertaken for German interests and there was little concern about the welfare of the occupied populations. German rule was designed to secure obedience to German wishes and to supply the German war machine. However, ultimately German occupation by German officials and troops was not popular and, as time passed and German fortunes began to wane, many came to question their collaboration. As we have said, in the east there was little scope for collaboration (except perhaps in the Baltic States); the Nazi approach was much more crude and designed to plunder, loot and enslave rather than strive for support. This ruthlessness threw away any possible economic and political benefits.

In general, resistance grew as the tide of war turned and the German authorities resorted to extreme measures to retain control – such as indiscriminate hostage-taking and retaliatory mass reprisals. The classic examples of this are the destruction of the village of Lidice in the Czech Republic in May 1942 after the assassination of Heydrich, Himmler's deputy, and the destruction of the French village of Oradour-sur-Glane in July 1944[2] – but these were only the more spectacular examples of what was a general policy – there were many more atrocities: in general the Germans executed ten civilians for each German killed. Of course resistance grew as the New Order became less attractive but in truth it was often neither wise nor practicable to do anything at all.

Certainly in Western Europe there were geographical problems as the terrain was not suitable for sustained partisan (i.e. guerrilla) activity. In fact resistance everywhere was generally a failure – the classic example being the disastrous Warsaw rising in 1944 where the

Poles rose up but were soon crushed and Warsaw destroyed (see pages 85 and 95). However, the situation was different in Russia where many Red Army soldiers were behind enemy lines, and in Yugoslavia where the mountainous terrain was a good place to conduct resistance.[3] Churchill set up the Special Operations Executive in 1940 to coordinate subversion and sabotage in occupied Europe, but most historians are of the opinion that it had little success. London felt intelligence work was the most useful activity for the resistance but results were limited. The French Resistance (also known as the Maquis[4]) is probably the best know resistance movement, but it was certainly not the most effective. In fact it only really came into its own in the summer of 1944 when it did make some positive contributions to the Allied invasion. Subsequently as the Germans retreated, everyone claimed to be in the resistance movement: the truth was rather different. More effective was the Italian Resistance movement. However, whatever we decide about resistance movements – and most historians believe they had a negligible impact on the outcome of the war – there is no doubt they played an important psychological role in covering up national shame and in creating the milieu for national reconciliation and the restoration of national respect.

For most people in Western Europe, German occupation was an unpleasant experience; however, for East Europeans it was far worse. East Europeans were considered by the Nazis to be sub-humans, suitable only for either exploitation or elimination.[5] However, this 'descent into barbarism' (MacKenzie) reached its nadir with the Nazi treatment of the Jews.

2 The Holocaust

> **KEY ISSUES** When was the decision for extermination made and who was responsible for carrying it out?

Anti-Semitism was not new but Hitler gave it a pathological dimension that defies comprehension. In origin anti-Jewish feeling was borne of religious animosity (the Jews were the murderers of Christ) but in modern times there was a strong element of jealousy at the success of Jews as entrepreneurs and intellectuals. Indeed what is quite remarkable is that they were condemned both for their capitalism and for their association with the origins of bolshevism. In Germany they were also made scapegoats for the defeat in the Great War. Nazi policy at first consisted of intimidation, persecution and legal discrimination and Jews were encouraged to emigrate. However, with the conquest of Poland (which contained 3 million Jews) and the widening war situation, the policy became one of systematic genocide that may have claimed the lives of as many as 6 million. The big questions surrounding this astonishing and horrific occurrence relate to the origins and timing of the killing (was liquidation the plan all along, as revealed in *Mein Kampf*, or was it an *ad hoc* response to the war situation?) and to responsibility for it (does Hitler bear the main responsibility or should it be more widely shared, by the Nazi party, the German people and their collaborators across Europe?).

Despite Hitler's speech in January 1939 prophesying the destruction of the Jews (see page 2), it does seem that the decision to initiate a 'final solution of the Jewish problem' was made in 1941 and coincided with the invasion of Russia. At first the Jews in Poland were herded into ghettos but as early as 1940 there was discussion of a final solution by Heydrich at the same time as there was a debate about resettlement in Madagascar – and a 'final solution' meant murder. Already the regime was eliminating undesirables via its euthanasia programme that had begun in October 1939, so the template for genocide already existed. The situation accelerated with the invasion of Russia: special SS killing squads (*einsatzgruppen*) followed the *Wehrmacht* east and systematically executed communist party officials and Jews – perhaps as many as a million, we cannot be sure. However, shooting was neither speedy nor efficient and Himmler himself found the process unpleasant.

Accordingly as early as the summer of 1941 plans were being drawn up for a more streamlined (and less public) method of liquidation and in September Russian prisoners-of-war were used as guinea pigs for the first gas executions at Auschwitz. In this sense the famous Wannsee Conference of 20 January 1942 was really *post facto* (after the event): the 'final solution' was already under way. However, the purpose of the meeting was to involve other government agencies in the process and extend it to all European Jewry. Thus death camps were established and the transportation of victims arranged. On arrival at the camps they were to be gassed by Zyklon B tablets and their bodies cremated. It was all arranged with unfeeling efficiency and carried out with ruthless brutality.

There can be no doubt that Hitler was behind all these developments: extermination was the logical consequence of Nazi ideology and the result of his pathological hatred of the Jews. The fact that there was no written order from him is neither surprising nor relevant – but the question is, how far should responsibility be shared? After all Hitler was not a man to get involved in the detailed planning and implementation of policy – there had to be a lot of initiative both at a high level and on the ground – from high ranking Nazis to lowly security personnel. Did the German people just look the other way or were they 'willing executioners'?[6] The argument that people did not know what was going on will not stand up, but it is clear that a population that has had its moral sensibilities blunted by war could only think of its own survival and had little time for the fate of the Jews. Few had clean hands – certainly not the *Wehrmacht* though there were of course decent people who loathed what was going on – but there was little they could do. And what of the occupied territories? Clearly there was considerable enthusiasm for this policy in both Vichy France and the Baltic states whereas in Denmark, Hungary and Italy there was resistance to it. However, when the Nazis occupied the last two the Jews were quickly rounded up and many were eliminated. Even the Allies did little to help. By the winter of 1942–3 there was knowledge of the camps, but what was going on seemed too fantastic to be believed. By 1944, however, what was happening could not be denied and yet incredibly the death camps were not targeted for bombing. The charge of moral myopia (short-sightedness) will not go away.[7]

Himmler ordered an end to the killing and the destruction of the camps in late November 1944 in the implausible belief that this might redound to his benefit at the end of the war! However, murder on such a scale could neither be covered up nor forgiven. Of course the great irony of the whole policy is that the Jews were a religious community and not a race at all! Quite how a civilised society could get caught up in such muddled thinking and crude barbarism remains an enduring and incomprehensible puzzle.

3 Technology and Intelligence

> **KEY ISSUE** Why did the Allies have the upper hand in technology and intelligence?

a) Technology

The Germans won the initial campaigns because of their superior air power and ground mobility, advantages they held in the first 3 years of the war, from 1939 to 1941. In order to beat the Germans the Allies needed to copy the Germans, and while it is easier to catch up than innovate, it is surprising that the Germans not only lost their lead but actually fell behind. Of course their failure to develop second generation weapons was largely due to the fact that they did not expect a long war.

Military historians are unanimous about the effectiveness of the German army and it remained a formidable fighting force until near the very end of the war despite material deficiencies. But the *Wehrmacht* never became fully mechanised and in tank warfare the Soviets soon proved to be more effective, producing good tanks in great quantities (e.g. the T34). The Germans responded too late with little coordinated planning. Their Panther and Tiger tanks may have been cutting edge technology but they were developed too late, in too few numbers, were rushed into production and proved very difficult to maintain.

In the air it is a similar story. In fact between 1939 and 1942 under the inept supervision of General Ernst Udet,[8] German aircraft development stagnated. Too many ambitious projects were started simultaneously, many of which ended up being impractical. Although the Germans did produce the very effective FW-190 fighter it is surprising that a state, which was renowned for its scientific and engineering ability, should have lost air superiority so rapidly in a war situation. Just as surprising is the recovery of the Soviet airforce, which (as with the army) had to start from scratch since its earlier obsolete equipment had been destroyed. The Soviets produced a number of very effective planes such as the Yak-9, which were more than a match for the ME-109. However, as we have already indicated (see page 68) the Americans produced the best all-round fighter in the Mustang.

German jet aircraft also came too late and in too few numbers to mount a serious challenge to Allied air superiority. For instance, the *Messerschmidt* 262 was not deployed until the spring of 1944 by which time the *Luftwaffe* was being eliminated as a credible force (see page 68). Similarly although the Germans pioneered rocketry, this also came too late to make a difference. The pilotless flying bomb (the V1) developed by the *Luftwaffe* did not launch until June 1944 and the missile developed by the army (the V2) was first launched in October of the same year. Production difficulties and Allied bombing not only delayed these weapons' deployment but also their production. Moreover, with the Allied advance launch sites were constantly pushed back. Despite Hitler's claims that his 'wonder weapons' would win the war they had very little impact on the outcome.[9] It is indeed fortunate that the one 'wonder weapon' that could have won the war, the atomic bomb, was not developed by the Germans. Hitler found the physics of the project difficult to grasp and showed little interest in something that was years away from realisation. It was seen as a post-war project (as it turned out to be in the case of the European theatre) and the German army gave up on it in 1942, though the programme continued. But for the Allies, who saw victory as a long way off, the bomb was a practical enterprise – inspired, ironically, by the belief that the Germans were well on the way to producing it. When Germany was finally defeated in 1945 it was estimated by Allied scientists that the Germans were still 5 years away from production – though protestations by German scientists that they had deliberately slowed the project on moral grounds seems unlikely given the fact that in some areas they were simply pursuing wrong solutions.

In terms of detection (radar) and counter-detection (jamming – blocking or interfering with signals) the Allies and the Germans were more evenly matched. Initially of course the British had the lead with radar, which played such an important role in the Battle of Britain (see page 21). Subsequently the Germans caught up and posed a major threat to the bombing campaign; however, from 1943 the Allies countered with WINDOW – dropping aluminium strips from aircraft, which completely foxed the radar. Electronic surveillance was also very important at sea and we have already seen how important huff/duff was in defeating the U-boat (see page 65). Once again German advances in submarine development came too late to make a difference. The pattern is clear: the Allies soon caught up and over-took the Germans who only woke up too late to the technological challenge. However, it is also clear that the Allies had far greater scientific and material resources for research and development.

b) Intelligence

The most successful aspect of the indirect war was not the sabotage and deception perpetrated by resistance fighters, but the work done by anonymous spies and cryptographers – and the work of the latter was understandably more important than that of the former. Of course there was some significant human intelligence, such as that provided by the Soviet spy Richard Sorge in Tokyo who enabled Stalin to shift forces from the east in the autumn of 1941 by reassuring him that the Japanese would not attack, but generally speaking intelligence from spies was marginal and patchy. All the German agents in Britain were discovered and many were turned into double agents and while the Russians probably had the most extensive network it seems they were most effective in spying on their Allies, Britain in particular!

The most important information was obtained by intercepting and decoding enemy signals, though the advantage between the Allies and the Germans went backwards and forwards for many years until the second half of the war when the Allies undoubtedly got the upper hand. Listening to German radio traffic (messages between the military), which was designed to go over a short distance, was in itself difficult and tedious work. The messages were then passed on to the code breakers at Bletchley Park. The Germans used a machine like a typewriter called Enigma containing about 200 keys, the codes for which were changed every 24 hours. Thanks to pre-war Polish intelligence and some brilliant mathematical minds it was possible to decipher the German messages. The resulting intelligence was called Ultra. The *Luftwaffe* codes were broken continuously from 1940; however, the Navy codes were more difficult to crack and the Gestapo impossible. This work provided high quality intelligence – it was authentic and uniquely credible – but of course it had its limitations. Sometimes the British decided to ignore the literal meanings of message because they seemed incredible. This was the case over the Battle of the Bulge in December 1944 – it was thought that the Germans were just too weak to launch an offensive. Sometimes it was just not possible to take advantage of the information – for instance, the British had advance warning of the German attack on Crete in 1941, but had insufficient forces in place to do anything about it.

Sometimes the information could be misinterpreted or underestimated; this was where intelligence officers came in – they could put together snippets of information and see the big picture. But overall the intelligence gleaned in this way played a most important role in the Allied war effort – in the Battle of Britain, in North Africa in 1942 (supply ships could be sunk and Monty knew Rommel's dispositions at El Alamein), in the Battle of the Atlantic (see page 61), and in the Battle for Normandy in 1944. Ultra sustained the confidence of the Allied decision makers and therefore played an important psychological role as well.

Another dimension of Allied intelligence was of course deception. We have already referred to the 'man who never was' (see page 57), but in the next chapter we will be looking at the most elaborate deception, Operation Fortitude, which was designed to persuade the Germans that the landing in Normandy was a feint and that the main invasion would come in the Pas de Calais area.

4 Alliances and Strategy

> **KEY ISSUE** Why did the Grand Alliance prove stronger than that of the Axis powers?

a) The Allies

i) The Big Three

The Grand Alliance that defeated Hitler was a remarkable thing. Capitalist America, Imperial Britain and Communist Russia were strange bedfellows. Indeed General George C. Marshall, Roosevelt's Chief of Staff, considered that their willingness to fight in a common coalition for so long was the single greatest achievement of the war. The leaders – the Big Three – were very different personalities but all three took a daily interest in the running of the war and were to some extent responsible for overall strategy. Of the three, Churchill was the only one who was technically not Commander-in-Chief, the king was, but that did not stop him acting as though he were. Churchill loved war, not in a bloodthirsty way but in the way a boy is fascinated by military matters; however, he made a number of strategic errors (e.g. over Norway and Greece) and it is fortunate that some of his wilder schemes were thwarted by his military advisers. In Sir Alan Brooke he had an outstanding Chief of the Imperial Staff. Roosevelt was Commander-in-Chief but he did not pretend to have a full grasp of military affairs and usually deferred to his advisers. He was in many ways a lofty idealist more concerned with post-war reconstruction and building a better world than involving himself in the strategy of particular military campaigns. Stalin was probably the sharpest of the three. He too was Commander-in-Chief but after his initial military mistakes in 1941–2 he was prepared to defer to his main generals Zhukov and Antonov, both of whom were outstanding.

Despite the fact that it was not always harmonious, Britain and America were able over time to develop a close working relationship built on an accumulation of trust. This was not the case with the USSR where the sheer distance and mutual suspicion prevented genuine cooperation. In many respects two separate campaigns were fought in Europe –but with one overarching aim: the defeat of Hitlerism. Thus the Grand Alliance was created by a common goal – by necessity rather than intention, and it held despite the strains.

ii) US Aid

The United States was alarmed by Hitler's success in 1940 and Roosevelt, re-elected that year on a platform of no war, decided to aid Britain by all means short of war. Although he saw Britain as a fellow democracy it should be remembered that there was no 'special relationship' at this time; Roosevelt himself was opposed to the British Empire (after all the USA had been a British colony) and was suspicious of Britain's aims. Still he agreed to a 'destroyers for bases' deal in October 1940, passed the Lend-Lease bill in early 1941 and extended convoy protection in May (see page 23). There were also secret military discussions and in June, when Hitler attacked Russia, Churchill and Roosevelt were quick to offer support, Churchill publicly, Roosevelt, for political reasons, more circumspectly – though in truth there was little the Allies could do for the Soviet Union in 1941.

Roosevelt and Churchill met off Newfoundland in August 1941 and issued the Atlantic Charter, which set out Allied war aims (even though the US was not at war!). This was the start of a very special relationship that proved to be of incalculable benefit to Britain and proved to be enduring. However, we must not exaggerate the warmth between the two men – there was mutual respect, but also differences and the relationship was often strained. In December, Japan attacked the US and although Roosevelt did not declare war on Germany, Hitler obliged a few days later.[10] Churchill was ecstatic and now believed victory was inevitable; without the USA and with the USSR seemingly on the verge of collapse this had not seemed likely before. Indeed the USA proved to be the 'arsenal of democracy' a phrase Roosevelt coined from a French politician, Monnet; the president set about mobilising the full industrial potential of America – the war would be won from the factories of Detroit. Despite his politics he brought opponents into his administration and allowed big business to just get bigger. In fact industrial production rose a staggering 96% during the course of the war. The federal budget, which was $9 billion in 1939, had ballooned to $166 billion by 1945. Not only did the Americans put well in excess of 8 million men under arms, but they fought two campaigns on opposite sides of the globe while supplying

Britain with 20% of her military equipment and the Soviet Union with trucks and rations for her soldiers. In fact American industry provided two-thirds of all the Allied military equipment produced during the war: 297,000 aircraft, 193,000 artillery pieces, 86,000 tanks, and 2 million army trucks. The American contribution to victory was truly awesome.[11]

FRANKLIN ROOSEVELT (1882–1945)

-Profile-

Born in New York, Roosevelt was educated at Harvard and subsequently became active in New York politics. He successively served as state senator (1910–13), and assistant secretary of the navy (1913–20), before becoming Democratic candidate for the vice-presidency in 1920. Following the disappointment of defeat at the polls, he was struck down by polio in 1921 at the age of 39. He suffered paralysis for 2 years and though he made a partial recovery he would be wheelchair-bound for the rest of his life. It is a measure of his determination that he recovered sufficiently to become the governor of New York, 1928–32, and his party's candidate for president in 1932.

He won the election by defeating Hoover and immediately set out to ameliorate the effects of the Great Depression by launching his innovative New Deal programme, which, among other things, involved state intervention in the credit market, agricultural price support and the creation of a social security system. He also repealed Prohibition. With his programme beginning to work, he was re-elected by a landslide in 1936, and again for unprecedented third and fourth terms in 1940 and 1944 respectively.

Ironically he was re-elected in 1940 because he was committed to keeping the USA out of the war. However, he modified his country's neutrality to favour Britain and later Russia, arguing that only by aiding them could the US avoid war! With the Japanese attack on Pearl Harbour and Hitler's declaration of war (both December 1941) Roosevelt was able to mobilise US resources for the defeat of both Hitlerism, his priority, and Japanese imperialism. He worked hard to achieve victory, appointed good military commanders and attended a number of meetings with Churchill (in particular) and also Stalin. The pressures created by both campaigning for his fourth term and the war put an inordinate strain on his health. After returning from Yalta in 1945 in an address to Congress he made the first and only public reference to his physical handicap in explaining why he was sitting rather than standing during his speech. Those who saw him during March were shocked by his frail appearance. His doctors pleaded with him to give up smoking, but he would not claiming it was one of the few pleasures left to him. He died 3 weeks before the Nazi surrender.

iii) Anglo-American Cooperation

The basic principles and overall strategy of the Anglo-American alliance were already in place prior to Pearl Harbour and were reiterated in a meeting in Washington that December when each of the 'United Nations' declared they would not make a separate armistice or peace. To his credit (and in opposition to his military advisers) Roosevelt stayed true to the agreed 'Europe First' strategy since he genuinely believed that Hitler was the greater evil. However, this was difficult to maintain as the Japanese threat seemed greater in early 1942 – moreover, the rapid success the US had in the Pacific later that year argued strongly for greater emphasis to be placed there. In truth there were greater numbers of US forces in the Pacific than Europe for practical reasons. Even in 1944, US forces were about evenly split between the two theatres.

In early 1942, a British staff mission was established in Washington DC and the Combined Chiefs of Staff was set up. Although Anglo-American cooperation was achieved by personal diplomacy at the top, it was held together by much more and there was considerable cooperation at lower levels where various joint boards and committees working under the auspices of the joint chiefs carried out their tasks with harmonious efficiency. Although individuals clashed (Field Marshal Montgomery was not particularly popular with the Americans) there was considerable mutual trust, respect and even friendship.

There was also a great deal of consensus about strategy – about defeating the U-boats at sea and about strategic bombing (though there was a different emphasis here – see page 67). Where the Allies did diverge was on the ground war. The Americans favoured the direct approach, an attack on Hitler's Germany and this coincided with Stalin's main concern. He constantly called for a second front and its constant postponement was a source of considerable ill will. Britain, however, favoured a more indirect approach in the Mediterranean where her campaign was ongoing and given the relative weakness of US forces at this time Churchill was able to dominate the strategic debate. He had enormous authority and despite setbacks his conduct of the war was remarkably uninhibited until it was curtailed by Britain's declining share of the war effort. A cross channel attack was deemed impractical in 1942, though if Russia seemed to be on the verge of collapse an emergency operation might be launched; however, the Americans insisted that absolute priority must be given to a cross channel invasion in 1943. A plan for the spring of 1943 was drawn up in the spring of 1942, this envisioned a million strong army, half of which would be American. The British agreed to this but then pressed for a combined North African operation, which seemed to render the 1943 invasion impractical. Against military advice Roosevelt agreed to Operation Torch (see page 56) though largely for political reasons; with Congressional elections looming large he wanted to be seen to be doing something. Churchill went to meet Stalin for the first time in August 1942 to explain the Mediterranean strategy. Although Stalin did not like what he heard, the two men got on and developed a measure of mutual respect.

Churchill and Roosevelt met again, in Casablanca in January 1943 where it was argued that the primary weapon against Germany was to be aerial bombardment pending the outcome of the Mediterranean campaign. The invasion of Sicily was also approved and Roosevelt coined the policy of unconditional surrender in a rather casual way at the press conference.

The Mediterranean strategy ruled out a cross-channel invasion in 1943. The defeat of the Germans in North Africa did not occur until May and Sicily was not invaded until July. As Mussolini fell, this then led on to the invasion of Italy though that campaign became bogged down (see page 58). In any event a cross-channel invasion in 1943 was not really practical. At the end of 1942, the Americans only had 170,000 troops in Britain and the demands of the Pacific and the continuing menace of the U-boats meant that a postponement had to be made. However, in Washington in May and in Quebec in August the Americans put their foot down: there had to be a cross channel invasion in the spring of 1944 – and it would be under an American supreme commander, Eisenhower. Churchill was not opposed to the invasion of France but he saw the Mediterranean campaign as a British one: he was proud of it and he knew that he would have to play second fiddle in Overlord. The postponement was even more of a disappointment to Stalin.

Indeed, distrust in the alliance became serious in 1943. In April, the Germans exposed the Russian massacre of 14,000 Poles at Katyn that had occurred during Soviet occupation. The US press became very critical and were quick to compare Stalin to Hitler. All this ill-will generated a real fear that Stalin might negotiate a separate peace. Moreover, he would not meet with Roosevelt and Churchill. They liked meeting for the sake of meeting – they believed in face to face contact and the development of personal relations. Stalin had no use for this – but once the tide had turned in the summer of 1943 he could come to a meeting in a much stronger position, and would be able to get his own way.

iv) Teheran and After
The first meeting of the Big Three then did not take place until the end of November 1943 in Teheran. Here Stalin proved to be much more professional, much better prepared than the democratic leaders who relied on the advice of subordinates for information that Stalin appeared to carry around in his head. At this meeting Churchill's stature was much diminished – although the prime minister was unwell, Stalin now had the upper hand in the east and the USA were coming to dominate the alliance in the west. Roosevelt was naïve enough to think he could manage Stalin when in reality it was the other way round. Stalin pandered to Roosevelt's vanity with respectful condescension, signed up to the United Nations (an international organisation planned as the successor to the ill-fated League of Nations) and agreed to go to war with Japan once German was defeated. He also favoured the invasion of France over a continuation of the Mediterranean strategy, though Russian survival was now no longer dependent on it. But what Stalin really wanted was territory, and in particular he wanted to control Poland. Churchill and Roosevelt went some way towards him on this, though everything was left deliberately vague.

In 1944 the Americans came to dominate the western alliance both in terms of contributing forces and determining strategy – thus the Mediterranean was relegated to the status of a sideshow and in France the broad front strategy was favoured over the British desire for a direct push to Berlin. There were other disagreements too over battle tactics in Normandy (see page 91), over the future of the Italian monarchy, over the composition of the Greek government and over continuing US aid under the terms of lend lease. However, the fissures appearing in the Anglo-American accord were nothing compared with the growing rift with the USSR. By 1944, Churchill was seriously worried about the post-war dominance of Europe by the Soviet Union. He was right to be concerned, but Roosevelt continued to place high hopes on his personal relationship with Stalin. He believed that because of the need for US aid, the post-war world would exist within an international democratic liberal economic structure. Because of this he was not as concerned as Churchill about the question of frontiers or the political complexion of regimes as perhaps he should have been. He clearly underestimated Stalin.

Stalin's cynical manipulation of the Poles in the Warsaw Rising of August 1944, where the Home Army was encouraged to rise up then was left to be slaughtered by the Germans, was something of a revelation. Poland had in fact become an embarrassment for the Western Allies and it was realised that concerns about the Polish government in exile – Polish leaders in London who expected to run the country after the war – and the frontiers created by the Nazi–Soviet Pact – the Soviets had taken a sizeable chunk of Poland in 1939 and did not want to return it – would have to be quietly forgotten. However, it was painful for the British to abandon the Poles – after all they were the reason Britain had gone to war but there was little the West could do; for Stalin Eastern Europe was non-negotiable. Even so Churchill flew to see him in October 1944 to try and get some limit on Soviet influence. In the so-called percentage agreements,[12] he at least kept the Soviets out of Greece and to some extent Yugoslavia – though the fate of Poland, Hungary, Rumania and Bulgaria was pretty much sealed. The Germans of course hoped that these differences would lead to a breakdown in the Grand Alliance but what they had forgotten was that hatred of Nazi Germany was the main reason for the alliance in the first place. There was no disagreement about the defeat of Germans, only about the consequences of that defeat. Obviously as the Allies came closer to victory, the more differences emerged, but no one lost sight of the ultimate goal.

v) Yalta

The Big Three met for the last time at Yalta in February 1945 by which time Roosevelt was dying (he died on 12 April). The Allies reached agreement on a post-war settlement for dividing up Germany and Stalin won concessions over Poland (though the Poles were be compensated for land lost to the Soviets in the east by gaining territory from Germany in the west). The sacrifice of the Poles has led many to describe Yalta as Churchill's Munich, but it is hard to see what the Western Allies could do; the political boundaries and complexion of Eastern Europe were going to be decided not by diplomatic negotiation but by the extent of the Red Army's advance.

Was Stalin driven by the need to spread communism or by concerns for security or indeed by old-fashioned nineteenth-century Tsarist expansionist aims? It would seem all three. In earlier years Stalin had pleaded for a second front – having survived and won he benefited from the delay for it gave him a mastery he might not have enjoyed had the Western armies been able to advance towards central Europe a year earlier. On the other hand, how many lives of British and American solders had been saved by the sacrifices of the Red Army? As we have suggested the campaigns of the Eastern and Western Allies owed little to one another – they were independent operations – and in these circumstances Allied cooperation became more political and less military, more concerned with the post-war settlement, less with the conduct of the war. Yet despite political differences the alliance held.

b) The Axis

If the Allies had difficulties in working together these were minimal compared to those of the Axis powers. Italy and Germany never really coordinated operations; Hitler and Mussolini had no wish to. In fact what joint action there was usually arose from Hitler saving Mussolini: in the Balkans and North Africa. In all these matters the Italians were either ignored or forced to submit to German command. At a personal level there was positive dislike – the Germans thought the Italians incompetent; the Italians thought the Germans arrogant. Hitler personally liked Mussolini but had little time for the Italian people whom he felt were unworthy of the *Duce*. Even so he did not inform Mussolini of Barbarossa and he ignored Mussolini's requests for a negotiated peace with Russia in the winter of 1942–3. For their part, and to their credit, the Italians ignored German requests to round up Jews. Eventually of course Italy switched sides and had to be occupied, as indeed were the smaller Axis allies such as Hungary and Rumania

Like the Allied leaders, Hitler was Commander in Chief of all the armed forces, but unlike the Allied leaders he chose to exercise increasingly close control, determining strategy and even the shape of particular operations. He took risks that his generals would never have taken and initially they paid off. Indeed his remarkable success before the war and for the first 2 years of the war put him in an unassailable position. In these years Hitler had allowed considerable local initiative (and indeed some discussion) within broad operational guidelines; however, the failure of Barbarossa at the end of 1941 produced a crisis, with Hitler firing those generals who counselled retreat. Henceforth all major operational decisions were made by the *Führer*, but he had no sense of his own limitations. Anyone who crossed him, he sacked, preferring loyalty to ability. He was not an administrator and there was no unity of command, no coordination of the services. His subsequent strategy seemed to consist solely of holding ground at all costs or attacking; most of his decisions after 1941 were bad ones. And he tended to interfere in small matters rather than see the overall picture. He became a lone commander, isolated in his headquarters or the Berghof, rarely making public appearances and at the end ordering the movement of armies that simply did not exist. His health deteriorated dramatically, particularly after the July Bomb Plot. He could no longer control his temper and his rages were accompanied by a trembling of the hands and feet. The shock of continuous defeats, the unhealthy life without fresh air or exercise and not least the poisonous drugs administered by his quack physician, Dr. Morrell, turned him into a physical wreck.

The Allied system was coordinated yet with a good deal of delegated responsibility. The Allied leaders certainly managed the war on a daily basis but committees spread the load over a wide administrative area. Moreover, as the war went on, military matters were handled more and more by the professionals. In Hitler's Germany the exact opposite occurred: Hitler's role got bigger and bigger and military matters came to be dominated by the will of one man. In this way he hastened defeat.

References

1. Over a million Poles were evicted from their homes.
2. Only 10 people out of a population of 652 survived: the men were shot and the women and children were locked in the church, which was burnt down.
3. Historians now feel that Tito's achievements have been exaggerated. It was the Russians who liberated Yugoslavia in September 1944 and it was only Stalin's surprising withdrawal that hid this fact.
4. The French word for bush or thicket
5. Of the 5 million Russian POWs, it is estimated 3 million died.
6. See especially Daniel Goldhagen, *Hitler's Willing Executioners* (Knopf, 1996) though the book has been criticised for going too far.
7. See Peter Calvocoressi, Guy Wint and John Pritchard, *The Penguin History of the Second World War* (Penguin, 1995), p.260, and also Alan Farmer, *Anti-Semitism and the Holocaust* (Hodder, 1998).
8. Udet actually committed suicide at the end of 1941.
9. Of course these weapons were not insignificant to the people of London and Antwerp who were underneath them.
10. Perhaps Hitler felt it was simply a gesture for Japan that (like Britain over Poland) would not have to be fulfilled?
11. See especially Richard Overy, *Why the Allies Won* (Jonathan Cape, 1995), pp. 190–8.
12. Stalin and Churchill decided that post-war influence could be represented in a mathematical way: thus Russian interest in Romania was put at 90%, western at 10; Hungary and Bulgaria were defined as 80/20; Yugoslavia 50/50 and Greece was deemed to be 90% western.

Answering essay questions on Chapter 5

i) 'Resistance was futile; collaboration the only option'. Did the peoples of occupied Europe have little choice but to obey the Nazis?

ii) 'Hitler had always planned to exterminate the Jews.' Is this a fair statement?

iii) 'Intelligence had only a very limited effect on the outcome of the war.' How far do you agree with this judgement?

iv) 'The Grand Alliance was a myth; self-interest was the only motive of the Allies'. How far do you agree with this judgement?

Once again remember that you can either agree or disagree with the proposition – or indeed settle for a middle way, provided you can justify your answer. And remember also to consider both sides of the argument. The second question is not just about World War Two – you are required to go back and consider *Mein Kampf*, Nazi anti-Semitic propaganda, discrimination from 1933, the Nuremberg Laws of 1935 and 'Crystal Night' 1938, as well as the events of 1939–41.

6 Total Defeat 1944–5

POINTS TO CONSIDER

This chapter outlines the end of the Third Reich. You should appreciate that the D-Day landings were not bound to succeed and that the Russians continued to make the major contribution to Nazi defeat.

KEY DATES

1944	6 June	D-Day landings in Normandy
	22 June	Operation Bagration: Soviet Offensive
	20 July	Failure of plot to assassinate Hitler
	1 August	Warsaw Rising
	15 August	Allied landing in south of France
	13–20 August	German forces destroyed in Falaise pocket
	25 August	Paris liberated
	30 August	Soviets enter Bucharest; Romanians switch sides
	September	Finland surrenders to Soviets
	17 September	Bulgaria overrun
		Failure to capture Arnhem
	October	British troops in Athens
	20 October	Belgrade liberated
	16 December	Battle of the Bulge begins
1945	January	Bulge closed by mid month
	12 January	Soviet offensive launched
	27 January	Soviet troops enter Auschwitz
	February	Budapest falls to Soviets
	7 March	Allies cross Rhine at Remagen
	22–26 March	Major crossing of the Rhine
	16 April	Battle of Berlin begins
	25 April	Berlin surrounded; US and Soviet forces meet at Torgau
	28 April	Mussolini killed by partisans
	30 April	Hitler commits suicide; Dönitz succeeds him.
	7 May	Jodl signs unconditional surrender
	8 May	VE Day; Keitel surrenders to Russians
	23 May	Dönitz government dissolved

1 D-Day and After

KEY ISSUE Why was Operation Overlord a success?

By the summer of 1944 the conditions were finally right to open the second front: the U-boats had been defeated, the *Luftwaffe* largely eliminated, the campaign in Italy and the east had drawn off many troops and the necessary numbers (7000) of landing craft were finally available (a not unimportant factor!). However, we should not allow hindsight to blind us to the uncertainty felt by contemporaries. The British were not confident of success and Churchill in particular had to be persuaded – it was really only pressure from Stalin that pushed him into full agreement with the Americans. In turn Hitler himself was confident of success; he believed a cross channel invasion could easily be repulsed, leaving him free to concentrate on the east and perhaps negotiate a settlement. After all, the Allied raid on Dieppe in 1942, which failed to get off the beach and resulted in considerable casualties, had been a complete disaster. Hitler knew the invasion was coming, but he did not know where or when. He sent Rommel to inspect the western defences, but by the time of the invasion his preparations were not complete. Still, the Atlantic Wall, a complex of shoreline obstacles, concrete bunkers and gun emplacements, was probably the most heavily defended coastline in Europe, and there were 60 divisions to back up the coastal fortifications.

Preparations for Operation Overlord, as it was called, were a year in the making, though an overall commander, Dwight D. Eisenhower, was not appointed until December 1943. Originally the plan had been to land three divisions, but both Eisenhower and Montgomery felt this should be raised to five to be preceded by three airborne divisions. The overall plan, the largest amphibious operation ever, ultimately envisaged the landing of nearly 2 million men. Normandy was chosen as the destination since the most obvious landing point with the narrowest crossing (the Pas de Calais) was the most heavily defended. Although the Normandy beaches did not have a port, the Allies overcame this problem by transporting two floating harbours (known as 'mulberries') and also laid oil pipelines under the ocean (PLUTO, 20 in all) – to ensure a speedy supply of fuel.

The whole operation was made possible by complete control of both the sea and the air (French communications were constantly bombed – railway lines in particular) as well as by an elaborate deception plan (Operation Fortitude) whereby the Germans were led to believe that the main attack was coming in the Pas de Calais area. To achieve this, an entirely fictitious army was simulated in south-east England, complete with dummy tanks and a credible commander (Patton), and 'revealed' to the Germans by phoney radio messages and false information from double agents. This was a complete success as the Germans were completely fooled. The bulk of their forces were in the north, though Runstedt and Rommel disagreed about their exact disposition. The latter believed the Allies should be defeated on the beaches whereas the former favoured holding forces back for greater mobility. However, mobility, as Rommel knew, was not practicable without air cover. Hitler intervened and pleased neither by diluting the forces and spreading them rather thinly.

D-Day (the 'D' stands for deliverance) was planned for 5 June, but atrocious weather conditions forced a postponement. However, there was a brief respite thereafter and so Eisenhower decided to go for it. On 6 June, the British and Canadians landed on the beaches designated Gold, Juno and Sword, and the Americans landed on Utah and Omaha. Only on the latter beach was there much resistance (the Americans ran into an infantry division on exercises and suffered 3000 casualties) and by the end of the day 156,000 Allied soldiers were ashore. The Germans responded slowly; because of the bad weather they were taken completely by surprise (in fact Rommel was in Germany for his wife's birthday!). Moreover, the destruction of communications immobilised the German forces, which were caught in the wrong place at the wrong time. In any case Allied air superiority (12,000 planes as opposed to a few hundred German) made movement by day impossible. However, what really slowed the German response was their continuing belief that the Normandy landings were a ruse and that the real attack would come at the Pas de Calais. It seems that it took them nearly 2 months to realise that this was not the case! Accordingly, the Allies were able to link up the landing points, move inland and reinforce: by 11 June, 326,000 troops were ashore, by the 14 June 557,000, by the 7 July a million.[1] The Americans moved into the Cotentin Peninsula and Bradley took the port of Cherbourg at the end of June (though it would not be fully operational for some time). However, German resistance stiffened and something of stalemate developed in July. Montgomery got held up before Caen and there were criticisms of his cautious approach; however, the British were facing the bulk of the German forces and providing a shield for the Americans in the west, who broke out under Patton at the end of July (Operation Cobra), occupying Brittany and swinging south to Le Mans.

Meanwhile the German High Command was rocked by an assassination attempt on Hitler on 20 July. On that day Colonel von Stauffenberg placed a bomb under the table in the conference room at the *Führer's* headquarters in East Prussia. It detonated, but the metal table took much of the blast and it only succeeded in destroying Hitler's trousers! He survived and took a terrible revenge. Once recovered Hitler turned his attention back to the western theatre and insisted on a counter attack in August. However, the *Wehrmacht* found itself caught between two pincers in the Falaise pocket (see Map 8) and even Hitler realised it was necessary to withdraw (16 August).[2] The Germans lost 60,000 men and most of their armour (by air attack as well as by ground forces) though an equal number escaped prior to the closure of the pocket. While this latter occurrence generated some criticism, the Falaise engagement was an important victory. The battle for Normandy was won – indeed the battle for the whole of

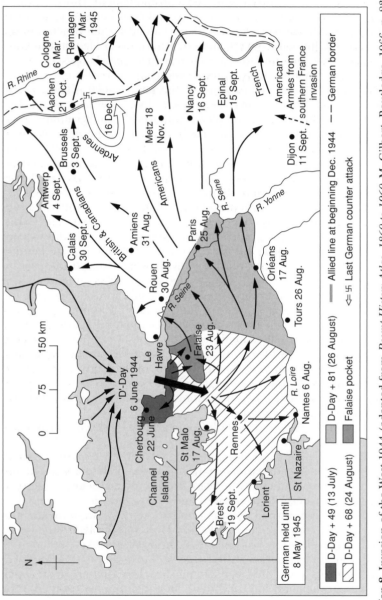

Map 8 Invasion of the West 1944 (adapted from *Recent History Atlas, 1860 to 1960*, M. Gilbert, Routledge, 1966, p. 83)

France was won, as the Germans now retreated back to the border. Meanwhile in the south there was a landing on the French Riviera on 15 August, which led to the capture of Marseille and Toulon.[3] Paris was liberated on 25 August – its capture was not part of the invasion plan, but Eisenhower feared its destruction (and possible capture by communist resistance fighters). Fortunately von Choltitz, the commandant of Paris, ignored Hitler's orders for the capital's destruction. De Gaulle, a stubborn and difficult man, and his Free French movement were allowed to carry out the liberation.

By the end of August the Allies had 2 million men in France (GB 830,000, USA 1.2 million), and at the beginning of September Montgomery liberated Brussels and Antwerp – indeed at this stage it looked as though the war might be over by Christmas, but it was not to be. Three factors militated against a quick victory.

For one thing the Allies were suffering from severe logistical constraints – it was very difficult to keep such a huge force supplied. Apart from the fact it took 4 months to get a tank from the US to France, the Allies only had the port of Cherbourg operational. Hitler ordered his forces to hold a dozen channel ports to the last man, and many were held until the collapse in May 1945. Antwerp was taken, but could not be used until the mouth of the Scheldt was cleared at the end of November (Monty undoubtedly missed an opportunity here).

Secondly, there were some strategic disagreements, mainly between Montgomery (a man who 'excelled in conceit ... and arrogance'[4]) and the Americans. Basically Montgomery wanted to undertake a rapid drive on Berlin while others wanted a more cautious broad front approach designed to take over the Ruhr, the Reich's industrial heart. Eisenhower believed a deep thrust could not be adequately supplied and therefore supported the broad front, though he did agree to Montgomery's ambitious plan (Operation Market Garden) to take the bridges at Nijmegen, Eindhoven and Arnhem by airborne assault (17 September). However, this operation went badly wrong at Arnhem and it was becoming clear that German resistance was stiffening.

This then is our third point: now that the Germans had retreated to the West Wall (or Siegfried Line), they regrouped, recovered and were prepared to defend the Reich. More than that, Hitler actually planned a surprise winter offensive.

Hitler's plan was to attack through the Ardennes, recapture Antwerp, split the Allies and roll them back into the sea. Hitler's generals thought this was somewhat over-ambitious; it was certainly a gamble and in reality it was the Führer's last throw of the dice. When the attack came on 16 December it was a complete surprise to the Allies. It should not have been, as Ultra decrypts had revealed an inkling of what was going on, but no one took the threat seriously. Hitler threw in 28 divisions, 200,000 men with 600 tanks, and the poor weather (mainly fog which eliminated Allied air superiority) enabled the panzers to make a quick advance. However, the Allies soon recovered and the Battle of the Bulge, as it became known, was soon over. The weather cleared on 23 December enabling the Allied airforce to attack the German advance; by Christmas the offensive was halted (it had only advanced 60 miles at its greatest extent and the Germans were short of fuel). By mid-January the bulge was closed. Montgomery's subsequent claim that he had saved the Americans did little to improve Anglo-American relations. The Germans had lost nearly 100,000 men and a great deal of new equipment that would probably have been better used on the Eastern Front. The Allies had suffered losses too, but unlike the Germans, theirs could be replaced. By now German industry was collapsing. In terms of strategy and morale, it marked the end of Germany's coherent resistance. It demonstrated to the German soldiers that the future held nothing but defeat. But the main consequence was that by committing Germany's last reserves to the Western Front, it guaranteed the Red Army a rapid advance in its winter offensive. Since the 6 June the Germans had lost over half a million men in the west and were now defending the Rhine. As Eisenhower pointedly said, 'the war was won before the Rhine was crossed'.[5]

2 Operation Bagration

> **KEY ISSUE** How significant was this largely unheard-of campaign?

Although there was not a great deal of military coordination between the Soviet Union and the Western Allies, Stalin did promise a summer offensive to coincide with the Allied landings in the west and he was true to his word. On 22 June 1944, the third anniversary of the launching of Operation Barbarossa, the Soviets launched Operation Bagration, so named after the Tsarist general who was mortally wounded at Borodino resisting Napoleon in 1812. This turned out to be Germany's biggest defeat of the war; however, its significance has to some extent been overshadowed by the western obsession with D-Day and the battle for France. Few of us have heard of Bagration and yet it eliminated twice as many Germans as the western campaign.

The Germans expected the Russians to press on with their offensive in the south, building on their previous success in order to overrun the Rumanian oilfields; accordingly they sent their reinforcements and much new equipment there, thereby denuding the central and northern fronts. However, the Russians planned an attack on Army Group Centre to eliminate the 300-mile salient there, push the Germans out of the Soviet Union and enter Poland. This was supported by a massive partisan operation in the German rear to paralyse the transportation system. Despite these activities German intelligence did not have an inkling about the operation and the *Wehrmacht* was taken completely by surprise. By concentrating their forces in one place the Russians enjoyed overwhelming odds with something like 1.5 million men and 4000 tanks up against 0.5 million Germans with only 600. Prior to the attack on 10 June there was a preliminary campaign against the Finns in the north, which ultimately led to their surrender in September.

When the Russian attack came, it was devastating. At the end of the first week the Germans had lost 200,000 men and hundreds of tanks; armies were enveloped, destroyed or forced to surrender. By mid-July the Soviets had advanced 200 miles and by the end of July the Red Army was at the gates of Warsaw. However, there it stopped and did nothing to help the Poles in the Warsaw Rising (Stalin allowed the Germans to slaughter the Polish Home Army since it fitted in with his plans to establish a communist regime there once the war was won).

Hitler's static defence and reluctance to withdraw gave the initiative to the Russians who extended the offensive to the north and the south. In the north there was a drive into the Baltic states – by September the Red Army had pushed the Germans out of Estonia, had cut them off in Courland in Latvia[6] and had driven into Lithuania, to the very border of the Reich itself. The attack in the south launched on 13 July had even more significant consequences as the invasion of Romania not only led to the loss of the oil fields, but to the destabilisation of Hitler's East European alliance system and his occupation of the Balkans. By the end of August, the Romanians were ready not only to surrender to the Soviets, but to switch sides which they duly did. This caused the Bulgarians to reconsider their position, but they dithered and were soon overrun by the Red Army in September.[7] These developments in turn compromised the German occupation of the Balkans and in September and October Hitler reluctantly agreed to withdrawal from Greece, Albania and southern Yugoslavia. Hungarian defection was only prevented by German occupation in October though the Russians had entered Hungary that month and by December had Budapest surrounded. An attempt by Slovakia to leave the Nazi fold was also crushed in October.

At this point we see a lull on the Eastern Front for about 3 months. Clearly the Soviets needed to regroup, reorganise their transport and replenish their supplies, equipment and manpower. However, nothing could hide the extent of German defeat – German casualties totalled nearly a million for the entire campaign and although resistance stiffened as the fighting approached the German border, the Red Army did enter East Prussia in October and were poised for a full scale invasion of the Reich itself.

Overall German losses in the summer and autumn of 1944 were colossal and irreplaceable. Taking all three fronts together they probably exceeded 1.5 million men and innumerable tanks and aircraft. If the military situation looked grim, the diplomatic situation was even worse, with the loss of Italy, Vichy France, Finland, Rumania and Bulgaria. Many neutrals were now hurrying to join the Allied cause while others like Spain, Sweden, Switzerland and Turkey were scaling down their supplies to the Reich. In Germany there was now great anxiety; the success of the western invasion, the success of the Russian offensive and the failure of the wonder weapons can have left few in doubt about the outcome. The employment of Germany's last reserves in the failed December offensive in the west and the collapse of Germany's industrial system accelerated by continuous Allied bombing set up Germany and her few puppet allies – Hungary, Slovakia, Croatia and Mussolini's social republic – for their final defeat.

3 Götterdämmerung[8]

KEY ISSUE Why did the Germans fight to the bitter end?

After the retreats of 1944, Hitler hoped to hold the Vistula in the east and the Rhine in the west, but by the beginning of 1945 the accumulation of Germany's reverses had produced growing disintegration. Still the Allies anticipated fierce resistance and though they did not coordinate their invasions, Eisenhower did appeal for an early Soviet winter offensive to take the pressure off the west where Hitler had launched his last major offensive. The Russians launched their winter offensive on 12 January 1945. By now they outnumbered the Germans by three to one, but by concentrating their forces they were able to simply overwhelm them. Hitler had denuded the centre by his strategy of holding on to parts of the Baltic and by sending his reserves to Hungary to protect his last remaining oil supplies.

Accordingly, when the Soviets attacked in the centre their 2.2 million soldiers were only faced by 400,000 Germans. Needless to say the Red Army smashed through Poland finally capturing Warsaw on 17 January and discovering Auschwitz on the 27 – in all they had advanced 300 miles by early February and were now standing on the banks of the Oder, only 45 miles from Berlin. East Prussia, Pomerania and much of Silesia were occupied while in the south, Budapest was taken in February and much of Hungary overrun. However, the final onslaught, the Battle for Berlin, was delayed until April (much to Zhukov's dissatisfaction) for a variety of reasons: Stalin wanted the flanks cleared of Germans, there were logistical difficulties, there were considerable preparations to be made and there was bad weather. The Russians needed to be sure of their arrangements for this final attack as they anticipated considerable resistance in the German capital.

Meanwhile in the west the 'Bulge' had been closed and the Allies were ready to go on the offensive. By early 1945 the Western Allied forces numbered a staggering 4 million men, and 2 million (of whom three-quarters were American), were now earmarked for the invasion of Germany. Prior to that though the Allies had to fight the Germans west of the Rhine. This Rhineland campaign occupied Eisenhower's forces from about 8 February to the 21 March and resulted in German losses of 350,000 (300,000 of whom were taken prisoner), losses that Hitler might have avoided had he allowed the troops to withdraw across the Rhine. The Allies were now poised to cross the river though famously the bridge at Remagen had been found intact on 7 March, enabling some US troops to get across already. The main crossings occurred later. Patton crossed on 22 March, and Montgomery on the 23rd and 24th – by the 26th there were 12 bridges operational. Eisenhower then instructed his armies to envelop the Ruhr from the north and the south thereby trapping German forces there: another 300,000 surrendered.

By now German resistance was collapsing though there were still pockets of fierce resistance, which made the advance sometimes unpredictable. Needless to say Montgomery, confined to northern Germany, wanted to play the leading role and to march on Berlin (and in this he was supported by Churchill ever fearful of Soviet advances), but Eisenhower resisted these entreaties. He knew that Berlin was going to be in the post-war Soviet zone and he knew its capture was going to be a bloody affair. Accordingly, he could not see the point and he assured Stalin, who was becoming overly suspicious at this time,[9] that the Red Army could have that particular prize. His concerns were military rather than political. British forces were to press on to the Danish border, US forces in the south headed for Bavaria[10] and Austria, and those in the centre pushed south of Berlin into Saxony where they met up with the Russians at Torgau on the Elbe on 25 April.

On the Italian front an offensive had opened on the 9 April; Bologna was taken on 21 April and by the end of the month the Allies were marching on Venice and Milan. On 28 April, Mussolini was shot by partisans while attempting to escape to Switzerland. Hitler meanwhile had confined himself (since the middle of January) to the bunker under the Chancellory in Berlin where his moods alternated between grim despair and hopes for a miracle.[11] Although he continued to issue a series of unrealistic operational orders, by April he knew that the end was not far off and ordered Germany's total destruction – an order that Speer disobeyed. The Führer was quite prepared to see Germany and the German people destroyed because, he felt, they had failed him – and yet many still obeyed and were loyal to him to the last. Of course most people were now more concerned with their personal survival, while others kept fighting believing that what might follow after surrender would be far worse. The rape and pillage perpetrated by the Red Army (and it was extensive[12]) was probably no worse than the treatment the Germans had meted out to the Russians just a few years before. The upshot was a mass exodus of refugees from the east to the west and the desire of many in the *Wehrmacht* to surrender to the Western Allies rather than the Soviets.

The Battle for Berlin finally began on 16 April. Stalin had promised Zhukov that he could take Berlin but he turned it into a race with Konev (Zhukov won). He gave them 2 weeks to finish the job – and that turned out to be about right. The Russians had overwhelming force – about 3 million men, 6250 tanks and 7500 aircraft. The Germans had about 3300 aircraft, 1000 tanks, little fuel and only about 320,000 soldiers; however, with the addition of *Volkssturm*,[13] Hitler Youth and others the total might have topped a million. Moreover, rubble-strewn Berlin was a big, sprawling city and the need to take it street by street and house by house (and come home alive) was not going to be easy. In the event the Red Army suffered over 300,000 casualties in this battle. Berlin was surrounded by 25 April and as the Soviets fought their way towards his bunker Hitler committed suicide there on 30 April. He appointed Grand Admiral Dönitz his successor and the Berlin garrison surrendered on 2 May.

The end when it came was understandably ragged. The first large-scale surrender came in Italy. The Germans there had been negotiating in Switzerland for a surrender solely to the west for some time but eventually they had to accept unconditional surrender to all the Allies. An Armistice was signed on 29 April and a capitulation on 2 May. Hamburg surrendered on 3 May and on the 4th, Montgomery accepted the surrender of German forces in Holland,[14] Denmark and north-west Germany. The Germans in Bavaria surrendered to the Americans on 5 May and by now the Russians were becoming suspicious, but Montgomery and Eisenhower would not agree to partial surrender despite Dönitz's attempts. Full unconditional surrender did not come until 7 May when Jodl penned the document at Eisenhower's headquarters in Reims; this had to be repeated for the Russians in Berlin by Keitel at midnight on 8–9 May. The Germans in Norway did not surrender until the 8th and over the next few days other pockets of resistance (e.g. the Channel Isles and the Baltic ports) finally capitulated. Dönitz's delaying tactics had enabled about 1.8 million of the Eastern Front army to become western POWs – about 1.5 million became Russian POWs. However, once resistance had ceased this government had outlived its usefulness and Dönitz and the other military leaders were arrested along with the top Nazis. Germany lay in ruins – she had suffered total defeat; there was to be no ambiguity about 1945 as there had been about 1918.

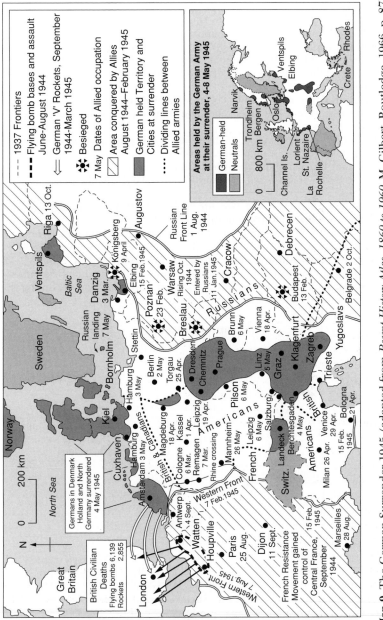

Map 9 The German Surrender 1945 (adapted from *Recent History Atlas, 1860 to 1960*, M. Gilbert, Routledge, 1966, p. 87)

References

1. It was not all plain sailing – on 19 June a storm destroyed one Mulberry and set the Allies back quite a bit.
2. We knew of his plans thanks to Ultra.
3. Marseille proved to be most important for supplies.
4. R.A.C. Parker, *The Second World War* (OUP, 1997), p. 204.
5. Quoted in Richard Overy, *Why the Allies Won* (Jonathan Cape, 1995), p. 179.
6. Many of these bases were held on to for the purposes of training U-boat crews.
7. Bulgaria had not actually declared war on the Soviet Union, as the Russians were fellow-Slavs. They had, however, declared war on Britain and America.
8. Literally means 'Twilight of the Gods' and is principally associated with Wagner's operas. It simply means the end.
9. He was worried about the Allied advance, worried that the Allies might take Berlin and worried that they would make a separate peace with the Nazis.
10. It was wrongly believed that the Nazis would make a final stand in a redoubt in the mountains of Bavaria.
11. The death of Roosevelt on 12 April brought a temporary bout of optimism.
12. See especially Antony Beevor, *Berlin; the Downfall* (Penguin, 2003).
13. A people's militia of old men and boys formed the previous September.
14. A deal to get food to the Dutch, many of whom had starved during the winter, was belatedly made on 30 April.

Summary Diagram

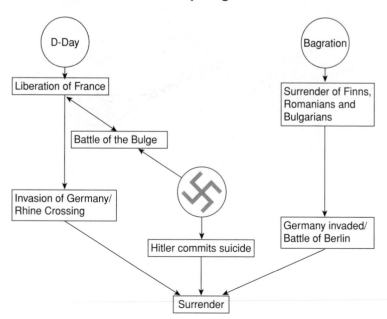

Working on Chapter 6

Notemaking

The contents of this chapter could be best summarised under the following headings – but be careful, there are a lot of facts in this chapter and you do not need them all in your notes. When it comes to answering essay questions, remember that factual detail is very important, but only in as far as it supports your argument:

Western Allies

i) D-Day – reasons for success
ii) Battle for Normandy and liberation of Paris
iii) No quick victory
iv) Battle of the Bulge

The Soviets

i) Bagration – reasons for success
ii) Destabilisation of Hitler's East European Alliance System
iii) German Losses

The End

i) Russia's Winter Offensive
ii) Rhine Crossings and Allied Strategy
iii) Reasons for German Resistance
iv) The Battle for Berlin
v) Surrender

7 Conclusions

POINTS TO CONSIDER

By way of conclusion it is worth considering again whether or not the Allied victory was bound to happen and also what the principal consequences of the war were.

1 Why the Allies Won

KEY ISSUE Was the Allied victory inevitable?

In his scholarly analysis of this topic,[1] Richard Overy makes the point that explanations of Allied victory contain a strong element of determinism – the Allies had superior resources, so were bound to win and did, etc. – but there was nothing predetermined about Allied success. The margin between victory and defeat was often slender. For instance, what would have happened if the *Luftwaffe* had kept bombing the RAF airfields in September 1940? And what would have happened if the Germans had correctly anticipated that the D-Day landings would take place in Normandy? Counter factual speculation has little validity in general, but it can sometimes give pause for thought and act as a check on any notions about historical inevitability. So, when it is suggested that by 1942, when Hitler found himself up against the combined resources of the United States and the Soviet Union, he could not win and his defeat was only a matter of time, we should be a little circumspect.

There is no doubting the material preponderance of the Grand Alliance. The combined industrial potential of the Allies far exceeded that of Nazi occupied Europe – despite the destruction of European Russia and US commitments in the Pacific. By 1943, Allied war production was three times that of the Axis (including Japan) and despite Herculean efforts directed by Speer in 1944 the Third Reich was still out-produced threefold in tanks and fourfold in artillery pieces – and Allied weaponry was not only superior, it was also actually relevant; German scientists might have been able to produce jet aircraft and rockets, but the army needed trucks. As late as 1944 the *Wehrmacht* was still relying on 1.5 million horses whereas the Allies were fully mechanised. Given the speed and scale of American rearmament and the swift revival of the Soviet economy it does look as though Hitler could not win. However, the material explanation is perhaps simplistic – look at the superiority of the French in Algeria in the 1950s, the Americans in Vietnam in the 1960s, or the Soviets in Afghanistan in the 1980s. In each case the greater power withdrew. As Professor

Overy has put it, the line from material resources to victory on the bat-
tlefield is not a straightforward one. The resources have to be
exploited effectively. Political will, technical modernity and a popular
willingness to accept sacrifices are just some of the many variables.

It was not easy for the democracies to turn civilians into warriors
but they did so. This was made easier by the fact that for the Allies –
their leaders, service personnel and their people – this was undoubtedly a just war. Nazism was a byword for inhumanity and many
believed that Hitler's triumph would herald a new dark age of barbarous cruelty. In addition, to a shared hatred of Hitlerism (and half
a century of anti-German feeling) was added the simple morality of
self-defence. Hitler aimed at conquest and domination. The Allies
believed they had right on their side and this moral conviction
engendered great confidence. The British responded to Churchill's
firm leadership and never looked like giving up. The Americans also
believed they were fighting evil, fighting for freedom – after all, they
were not fighting for survival. The Russians, on the other hand, most
certainly were. The brutality of the German onslaught and Stalin's
recourse to traditional patriotism (as well as traditional coercion) produced an astonishing response from the Russian people who showed
a remarkable capacity for sustained sacrifice on an unbelievable scale.
The notion that the war embodied Good versus Evil may be too
simple given the nature of the Soviet regime on the Allied side, but
the Western Allies certainly believed that Hitlerism was a much
greater evil than communism, and few would disagree.

The Germans also showed a willingness to fight – though not from
the moral high ground. The Axis populations knew theirs was a war
of aggression and as the tide turned there was growing disillusion and
many uneasy consciences. Still, belief in the *Führer*, strict discipline
and, above all, the fear of defeat kept a considerable number of
Germans fighting until the bitter end.

However, the Allies had better leaders and better decision-making
processes. Hitler made decisions based on false racial and social
assumptions about the enemy (e.g. the Americans were decadent, the
Russians inferior, etc.) and he distrusted professional advice. The
Allies on the other hand had civilian leaders who were prepared to
listen to advice and they developed elaborate bureaucratic mechan-
isms run by experts. In fact the Allies were better at planning, better at
logistics and better at mobilising the civilian population to assist in the
war effort. Eventually they were also better at fighting, though no one
underestimates the immense fighting capacity of the German army.

So, what is more important – material factors or human factors?
Despite material superiority, if the Allies had been divided, demoralised and badly led, they would probably have lost. But in the event
they were not – they were well led and well resourced, with both the
latest weaponry and with supportive populations who believed in the
justice of their cause. When horrifying newsreels of the liberation of

the concentration camps fully revealed the true nature of the Nazi regime, the rightness of this belief was doubly confirmed.

Accordingly between 1942 and 1944 the Russians got the better of the *Wehrmacht* and the Western Allies defeated the U-boat and achieved air superiority over the *Luftwaffe*. Why the Allies won is a complex story simply because there are so many factors that account for it, but it is clearly a combination of superior human *and* material resources. It is obvious that Britain could not have won without American aid – but equally obvious that the Western Allies could not have won without the enormous sacrifices of the Red Army. After the war Stalin suggested that in the cause of victory Britain had provided the time, America the money and Russia the blood – and there is some truth in this.

2 Consequences

KEY ISSUE What were the principal effects of the war?

a) Death and Destruction

The most obvious consequences of the Second World War were death and destruction; there had been suffering on an unprecedented scale. It was quite simply the most devastating conflict in human history. Estimates of the number of deaths are notoriously difficult to arrive at, but the general view is that in all over 50 million persons died (this includes the Pacific theatre). The Russians did most of the dying; figures of up to 25 million (over two-thirds of whom were civilians) are probably not an exaggeration. There were possibly about 6 million deaths in Poland, half of whom were exterminated Jews; proportionately this was the greatest number. The Germans suffered about 4 million deaths, three-quarters of whom were in the armed services, and Yugoslavia may have suffered anywhere between 1 and 2 million. The number of fatalities in the west (including the USA) were probably about 1.5 million in total; for Britain and France this was a lot less than the First World War but a considerable sacrifice nevertheless. In all some 6 million Jews were killed. In addition, there was a huge displacement of peoples, possibly some 25 million principally Germans and Poles who were forced west; many Baltic peoples were deported east.

The physical destruction was on an equally colossal scale – 1000 square miles of Russia were laid waste. Many cities were destroyed by bombing or battle and towns and villages had disappeared. Factories were destroyed, as were communications – bridges, railways – too. Agriculture was devastated; animals were killed and equipment destroyed. Europe was prostrate.

b) Victory Vindicated

Was it all worth it? This seems a strange question to ask particularly in view of the fact that the majority of participants had no choice – but we have to consider the alternative. Hitler's desire for world domination and a racial empire threatened everyone. Indeed, the Nazis were a threat to all civilisation and their triumph would have led, as we have said before, to a dark age of barbarous cruelty. The Nazi leaders were brought to trial in Nuremberg in November 1945 and while there have been philosophical arguments about the legality of the victors trying the vanquished, there has been little debate about the verdicts.[2] What debate there has been often relates to the fact that too many guilty men either got off lightly or got off altogether. Against the argument (favoured by Churchill) that the Nazi leaders should have been shot out of hand is the fact that the 9-month trial was able to reveal the full horror of the Nazi regime for all to see.

c) Cold War

The war did not end with a peace treaty – after all there was no German government to negotiate with. Germany was divided into four occupation zones – British, American, French and Soviet – as was Berlin though it was deep inside the Soviet zone. By the end of the war the relations between the Allies were deteriorating fast: what had held them together – the common hatred for Hitler – was no more. Because the Soviet Union had been essential to Allied victory there had been a tendency to gloss over the unpleasant nature of the regime. The moral ambiguities in the Allied coalition were never strong enough to undermine the image of a righteous cause. But with the common enemy removed, the anti-communism of the democracies could now be expressed – in a sense the Cold War was a resumption of relations as they had been prior to 1941. Already, relations had deteriorated over Poland. When various members of the 'Big Three'[3] met at Potsdam, in July and August 1945, the Soviet Union continued to affirm its commitment to free elections and democracy, but Stalin would not be deflected from turning the East European states into communist satellites. Everywhere the Red Army was – in Poland, Hungary, Bulgaria (1946–7) and later Czechoslovakia (1948) – one-party regimes emerged, and there was nothing the western leaders could do about it. The United Nations Organisation set up in 1945 to, among other things, perpetuate the Grand Alliance, became a forum for confrontation as the world slipped into the Cold War. In 1946, Churchill spoke of an Iron Curtain descending across Europe – and the geo-political divide between east and west remained set in roughly the place where the Allied armies had halted in 1945. The Cold War was to last for nearly half a century, but at least it did not lead to another war. Seen from the perspective of the 1980s, this bipolar world in which two ideologically opposed power blocs faced each other, appeared to be the most obvious consequence of the Second World War, but now it has passed we can view it as a temporary occurrence – though what has taken its place is less easy to define.

d) The Superpowers

Undoubtedly the USA and the USSR emerged from the Second World War as superpowers; in order to deny Germany's bid for world power, the USSR and the USA had to become world powers themselves. The USA emerged as 'the most powerful nation in the world' to quote President Truman,[4] able to out-produce all the other powers put together. The US homeland had not been touched by war; her economy had been boosted by it and her achievement in putting 15 million people under arms and in effect fighting two wars was remarkable. She emerged as not only the mightiest power, but as a nuclear power as well. Moreover, the USA has maintained this position to the present day.

Victory gave communism a new lease of life sustained by Soviet military power. The Soviet Union was undoubtedly a military superpower but her economy remained backward. There was to be no economic miracle in Russia – the system could not even provide a decent standard of living for its people – and eventually it could not even afford to sustain its military capability. Since 1991 communism has gone from Europe and the Soviet Union has fallen apart. The unfortunate Soviet people won neither freedom nor prosperity for their efforts, but it should be remembered that it was their sacrifices that made it possible for many of the other warring states to enjoy them both.

e) Britain and the European Powers

For Britain the war was a disaster – she lost her Empire and her world role, though many would argue that the war simply accelerated a process that was already in train. In 1945 she faced a 'financial Dunkirk' in the words of Keynes[5] and was reduced to the status of an American pensioner. Decolonisation was not just a consequence for Britain but for the French and the Dutch too. These states looked more to European cooperation for their future. Indeed in many ways the European Union was a consequence of the experience of the Second World War, an attempt to stem the rivalries and ambitions of the European powers by merging them into a cooperative body.

Given the condition of Russia and Britain, there is a certain irony in the fact that Germany and Japan made remarkable economic recoveries in the post-war period (largely due to US assistance in the initial stages). This of course has led cynics to pose the question about who had actually won the war. However, both Germany and Japan have renounced militarism and are no longer a threat to their neighbours. Indeed the ability of most European states to provide its populations with reasonable prosperity without the conquest and exploitation of others has made the prospect of another European war seem quite inconceivable from present perspective. No one claimed at the end of the Second World War as they had at the end of the First, that this was a war to end all wars but let us hope it was the last world war. After all, the development of the atomic bomb has ushered in a new, nuclear era in which the next world war would undoubtedly be the last.

References

1. Richard Overy, *Why the Allies Won* (Jonathan Cape, 1995).
2. Twenty-two in total were tried for 'crimes against humanity', 'causing war' etc, one in absentia (Bormann) – 12 received death penalties; three, life sentences; four, between 10–20 years and three were acquitted. The US, British and French held their own trials - as did Israel and Germany later. See Peter Calvocoressi, Guy Wint and John Pritchard, *The Penguin History of the Second World War* (Penguin, 1995), p. 573.
3. Truman who had succeeded Roosevelt in April, attended both, as did Stalin. Churchill attended in July, but was succeeded by Attlee who defeated him in the election.
4. Quoted in Overy, p. 327.
5. Quoted in Martin Kitchen, *A World in Flames* (Longman, 1990), p. 337.

Summary Diagram

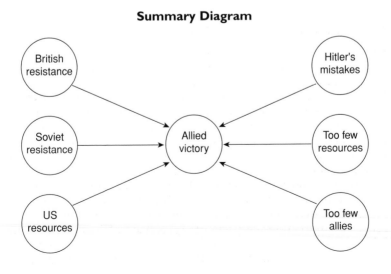

Working on Chapter 7

The really important question about the Second World War is of course why the Allies won. Indeed did the Allies win or did Hitler lose? The answer is potentially huge, but the examination question will guide you into focussing on one particular aspect, perhaps in a particular period. This does not mean you can ignore the other factors, but it does at least channel your thinking. For example:

1. To what extent were strategic mistakes by Hitler from 1941 responsible for the defeat of Germany in the Second World War?
2. To what extent was Germany's decline and defeat in the years 1943–5 due to the impact of US intervention?

Quite clearly in question one you must write about Hitler's mistakes at some length, before going on to mention other factors such as the fighting ability of the Red Army or the massive resources of the USA. Similarly in the second question, your focus must be on the US contribution, but you should not confine yourself to it – and you certainly do not have to agree with the proposition – provided you can back up an alternative explanation. With the 'To what extent' questions examiners are primarily looking for a balanced answer that discusses the question's suggested explanation but also weighs up other factors. You should look back at the mark scheme outlined on page 28 for guidance. Remember you must always address the question; your answer has to be an argument, not a narrative of 'all the facts I know on this topic'.

Further Reading

There are literally thousands of books on the Second World War. Amazon.com lists nearly 20,000 on the UK website alone, ranging from broad outlines to detailed analyses of particular battles. Single volumes came out in large numbers in 1989 to coincide with the 50th anniversary of the war's outbreak. However, possibly the best came out a little later:

Gerhard L. Weinberg, *A World at Arms* (CUP, 1994). This book is nearly 1200 pages long, has a bibliographic essay (24 pages), a full and informative set of notes (180 pages) and covers the Pacific as well as Europe (as do all these works unless otherwise stated). If this represents too formidable a work, there is a more compact and more recent single volume:

A.W. Purdue, *The Second World War* (Macmillan, 1999). At just over 200 pages this is probably a more realistic next stop after this book.

Other single volumes include:

Peter Calvocoressi, Guy Wint and John Pritchard, *The Penguin History of the Second World War* (Penguin, 1995). Since 1972 this book has had several incarnations as one or two volume works. It was extensively revised in 1989, runs to over 1300 pages and contains some excellent maps.

R.A.C. Parker, *The Struggle for Survival* (OUP, 1989). This was renamed *The Second World War* in 1997 and has been favourably reviewed. It is a masterpiece of compression covering all aspects of the war in just over 300 pages and yet contains much detail and analysis.

John Keegan, *The Second World War* (Hutchinson, 1989) – a good read.

Martin Kitchen, *A World in Flames* (Longman, 1990). This just missed the 50th anniversary and is now only available via Pearson Print on Demand.

S.P. Mackenzie, *The Second World War in Europe* (Longman, 1999) – this work is confined to Europe, but is not very detailed; however, it does contain 25 documents at the back.

Also recommended are:

H.P. Willmott, *The Great Crusade* (Michael Joseph, 1989).

Martin Gilbert, *The Second World War* (Weidenfeld and Nicolson, 1989). This adopts an unusual almost day-by-day approach.

Older 'coffee table' books that are still useful include:

A.J.P. Taylor (ed), *History of the Second World War* (Octopus, 1974)

E. Bauer, *The History of World War II* (Orbis, 1979)

A more recent 'coffee table' book is the relevant volume in the Cassell History of Warfare series, which contains lots of maps and illustrations:

Charles Messenger, *The Second World War in the West,* (Cassell, 1999).

For reference the best work is:

I.C.B. Dear and M.R.D. Foot (eds), *The Oxford Companion to the Second World War* (OUP, 1995). This contains over 1750 alphabetically arranged entries written by over 140 contributors.

Last but not least:

Richard Overy, *Why The Allies Won* (Jonathan Cape, 1995) – a thought-provoking reappraisal (see Chapter 7)

All of these books contain extensive bibliographies that deal with works on the various countries, political leaders, generals, military campaigns, economics, intelligence and the holocaust.

Dramatis Personae

ALANBROOKE, Alan Brooke, Viscount (1883–1963) He rose to be a general staff officer in World War One and commanded a corps of the BEF in France 1939–40, covering the evacuation from Dunkirk. He became commander-in-chief of the Home Forces and then, in 1941, chief of the Imperial General Staff (CIGS) to 1946. As such he was Churchill's principal strategic adviser and accompanied him to all the important summit meetings. His war diaries proved controversial.

AUCHINLECK, Sir Claude (1884–1981) He served in the Middle East in the First World War and was involved in the Norwegian campaign in the Second, before becoming commander-in-chief in India (1941). In the same year he succeeded Wavell in North Africa. His successful advance was reversed by Rommel in 1942 and, though he regrouped at El Alamein, he was made a scapegoat for the retreat and was replaced. In 1943 he returned to India as commander-in-chief. In 1946 he became a Field Marshal.

BADOGLIO, Pietro (1871–1956) He served in the Italian army in the First World War and was made a Field Marshal in 1926. He directed the campaign in Abyssinia (1935–6) and in 1940 was made commander-in-chief but resigned after the failure of the Greek campaign. After Mussolini's fall, he formed a government that signed an armistice with the Allies and declared war on Germany. He resigned in 1944.

BRADLEY, Omar (1893–1981) A graduate of West Point, the USA's premier military academy, he served in the First World War and in 1941 commanded a corps in Tunisia and later Sicily. He commanded US forces at the Normandy invasion in 1944 and later the 12th Army Group through France. In 1950 he became a five star general.

BRAUCHITSCH, Walter von (1881–1948) He served in the First World War and in 1938 became commander-in-chief of the *Wehrmacht*. He was promoted to Field Marshal after the successful campaigns in Poland and the west. He was relieved on health grounds in 1941 when Hitler made himself commander-in-chief. He died of a heart attack just prior to being brought to trial by the Allies.

CHURCHILL, Sir Winston (1874–1965) See the Profile on page 18.

CLARK, Mark (1896–1984) He graduated from West Point and was wounded on active service in Europe in the First World War. Prior to Allied landings in North Africa in 1942 he secretly landed in Algeria and narrowly escaped capture. He commanded US forces at the Salerno landing (1943) and Anzio and captured Rome in 1944. In 1945 he commanded US forces in Austria and later served in Korea.

DE GAULLE, Charles (1890–1970) He fought in World War One and in 1940, with the fall of France, he fled to England where he raised the standard of the 'Free French'. Entering Paris at the head of the earliest liberation forces in 1944 he became head of the provisional government. He later withdrew from politics but returned as President 1958–69.

DÖNITZ, Karl (1891–1980) See the Profile on page 62.

DOWDING, Hugh, Baron (1882–1970) He joined the Royal Flying Corps in World War One and was decorated for his service. As commander-in-chief of Fighter Command (1936–40) he organised the air defence of Britain. Despite success in the Battle of Britain he was relieved of his post in November 1940. Before he retired he was created a peer in 1943 and later became interested in spiritualism.

EISENHOWER, Dwight (1890–1969) See the Profile on page 56.

GAMELIN, Maurice (1872–1958) He served in the French army in the First World War and his seniority brought him the post of chief of staff in 1935. 1940 disproved his pronouncement that to 'attack is to lose' and he was hurriedly replaced by Weygand. In 1943 he was tried by Vichy and imprisoned until 1945.

GOEBBELS, Josef (1897–1945) After attending eight universities he became an enthusiastic supporter of Hitler and edited the Nazi newspaper. In 1933 he was appointed Minister of Public Enlightenment and Propaganda. Wartime conditions greatly expanded his responsibilities and by 1943 he was virtually running the country while Hitler concentrated on the war. He committed suicide with the *Führer* in the bunker in Berlin in 1945.

GOERING, Herman (1893–1946) He became a flying ace in World War One and later joined the Nazi Party (1922). He was in charge of the SA for a while and became a Reichstag deputy in 1928. Later in 1932 he became President of the Reichstag before holding several posts in the Nazi government, founding the Gestapo, organising the economy and running the *Luftwaffe*. Failure against Britain and mounting Allied air attacks led to a loss of prestige. In 1946 he was condemned to death at Nuremberg but escaped the noose by committing suicide.

GORT, John,Viscount (1886–1946) He served in World War One and was awarded the VC in 1918. In World War II he was the commander-in-chief of the British forces overwhelmed in 1940. He later served in Gibraltar, Malta and the Middle East. He was made a Field Marshal in 1943.

GUDERIAN, Heinz (1888–1954) A leading tank expert he created the panzer armies that overran Poland in 1939 and France in 1940. Recalled after the failure to take Moscow in 1941, he was chief of general staff in 1944 and later commander on the Eastern Front.

HALDER, Franz (1884–1972) A career soldier who served in World War One, he became army chief of staff in 1938. He remained involved in military planning until 1942 when he disagreed with Hitler over the Stalingrad campaign and was dismissed.

HARRIS, Sir Arthur (1892–1984) He joined the Royal Flying Corps in World War One and by 1937 was an air commodore. As commander-in-chief of Bomber Command RAF (1942–5) he earned the nickname of 'Bomber Harris'. He is still a figure of controversy (see page 66).

HEYDRICH, Reinhard (1904–42) Originally in the Free Corps, he joined the Nazis and rose to be second in command of the secret police. In 1941 he was made deputy-protector of Bohemia and Moravia and was involved in decisions leading to the 'Final Solution'. In 1942 he was assassinated and the Czech village of Lidice was destroyed (along with every male inhabitant) as a reprisal.

HIMMLER, Heinrich (1900–45) An early Nazi, he participated in the Munich Putsch (1923). In 1929 he was put in charge of the SS (*Schutzstaffel*: protective force) Hitler's personal bodyguard, which he developed into a powerful group. Inside Germany and later in war-occupied countries he used the SS and Gestapo to unleash a terror campaign that culminated in genocide. In 1943 he was made Minister of the Interior and in 1944 he was made commander-in-chief of the home forces. He was captured by the British at Bremen but avoided execution by committing suicide.

HITLER, Adolf (1889–1946) See the Profile on page 2.

JODL, Alfred (1890–1946) After being wounded in the First World War he became a staff officer and was named chief of the armed forces' operations staff in 1939. He was Hitler's closest military adviser and as such signed many orders that sanctioned military atrocities. He signed the surrender in the west in May 1945 and was executed at Nuremberg for war crimes.

KEITEL, Wilhelm (1882–1946) He served in the artillery in the First World War and became an ardent Nazi in the 1930s. In 1938 he was appointed chief of the supreme command of all the forces and in 1940 he signed the armistice with France. Throughout the war he was Hitler's chief military adviser and in 1945 he signed the surrender in Berlin. He was executed at Nuremberg for war crimes.

KESSELRING, Albert (1885–1960) After serving in the army in World War One and Weimar, Kesselring transferred to the *Luftwaffe* after Hitler's accession to power. He commanded air fleets in Poland in 1939 and in France and in the Battle of Britain in 1940. Late in 1941 he became Commander-in-Chief South, and after the Allied invasion of Italy fought a solid defensive campaign. In March 1945 he was appointed Commander-in-Chief West, but he was unable to prevent the German surrender in May. In 1947 he was tried for war crimes but released in 1952.

KONEV, Ivan (1897–1973) He served in the artillery in the First World War and became a military commissar after the Revolution. From 1942 he held several commands and was instrumental in pushing the Germans out of the Ukraine. After the war at various times he commanded the Soviet Army, the Warsaw Pact and was deputy defence minister 1946–60.

MANSTEIN, Fritz von (1887–1973) He was chief of staff in the Polish campaign and later the architect of Hitler's victory in France in 1940. He served on the southern flank of the Russian front and handled his panzers with great resource both in attack and in retreat. He was relieved of his command in 1944, captured in 1945 and imprisoned until 1953.

MARSHALL, George (1880–1959) After being commissioned in 1901 he rose to the highest rank and as chief of staff (1939–45) he directed the US army throughout World War II. After the war he became secretary of state and initiated the aid programme that bore his name. He was awarded the Nobel Peace Prize in 1953.

MODEL, Walther (1891–1945) He served in Poland, France and on the Russian front. His skill in defence was recognised when he was given a series of senior but doomed commands in 1944–5. He committed suicide in the Ruhr pocket just prior to the end of the war.

MONTGOMERY, Bernard, Viscount See the Profile on page 55.

MUSSOLINI, Benitio See the Profile on page 24.

PATTON, George (1885–1945) He graduated from West Point in 1909 and commanded an armoured brigade in World War One. In 1941 he commanded a corps in Africa and the US 7th Army in Sicily. Later as the head of the 3rd Army he swept across France and Germany 1944–5. A flamboyant commander, he was known as 'Old Blood and Guts'. He died in a car crash in Germany just after the end of the war.

PAULUS, Friedrich von (1890–1957) As commander of the VIth army he capitulated to the Russians at Stalingrad in February 1943. Released from prison in 1953 he became a lecturer in communist East Germany.

PÉTAIN, H. Philippe (1856–1951) By 1916 he was in command of an army corps and his heroic defence of Verdun ('they shall not pass') made him a national hero. He became commander in chief of the French army in 1917. After the war he championed the Maginot Line and after France's defeat in 1940 he became the head of the government at the age of 84. He signed the armistice with Germany and his government at Vichy became the byword for collaboration. With liberation he was tried for treason but his death sentence was commuted to life. He died in captivity.

QUISLING, Vidkun (1887–1945) Norwegian fascist leader, he became the Germans' puppet prime minister in occupied Norway. In 1945 he gave himself up and was tried and executed. His name has become a byword for traitors.

RAEDER, Erich (1876–1960) He entered the navy in 1894 and was chief of staff in the First World War. In 1920 he was promoted admiral and became commander-in-chief of the fleet. Under Hitler he built up the navy but in 1943 he was dismissed over strategic disagreements. He was sentenced to life at Nuremberg but was released in 1955.

ROMMEL, Erwin See the Profile on page 53.

ROOSEVELT, Franklin See the Profile on page 82.

RUNSTEDT, Gerd von (1875–1953) He served in World War One rising to Chief of Staff. At the outbreak of the war in 1939 he directed the *blitzkrieg* in Poland and France but was relieved of his command in the Ukraine in 1941. In 1942 he was appointed Commander-in-Chief West, but was relieved of his command and then re-appointed (both in 1944) to lead the Battle of the Bulge. Once again he was relieved of his command and he was captured in May 1945 but released on grounds of ill health.

SPEER, Albert (1905–1981) He joined the Nazi Party in 1931 and became Hitler's chief architect in 1934. In 1942 he was appointed Minister of Armaments and his talent for organisation resulted in greatly improved industrial production. The only Nazi leader at Nuremberg to admit guilt, he was sentenced to 20 years' imprisonment.

STALIN, Josef See the Profile on page 34.

TIMOSHENKO, Semyon (1895–1970) Born of peasant stock he was conscripted into the army in 1915 but after the Revolution joined the Red Army and fought in the Civil War. With the German invasion he took command in the Ukraine but was unable to stem the Nazi tide. He then moved to the northern front and was later (1943–5) Stalin's personal representative on several fronts.

WAVELL, Archibald, 1st Earl (1883–1950) He was commissioned in 1901 and served in the Boer War. He was wounded in the First World War and became Chief of Staff in Palestine. From 1938 to 1941 he was commander-in-chief of British forces in the Middle East and as such had great success against the Italians. But he was defeated by Rommel and transferred to the Pacific in 1943.

WEYGAND, Maxime (1867–1965) He was chief of staff to Foch (1914–23) and chief of staff of the army (1931–5). In 1940 he was defeated by the Germans and captured. Later he was allowed to retire in obscurity.

ZHUKOV, Georgi See the Profile on page 42.

Index